Neugierig?
Dann treten Sie ein ...

... in ein neues Lernerlebnis!

Grammatik üben mit Bildern – warum?

Einer der Gründe sind Sie selbst und wahrscheinlich auch die Motivation, aus welcher heraus Sie dieses Buch in den Händen halten!

Die meisten Menschen, die eine Sprache lernen, kommen nicht darum herum, sich mit Grammatik zu beschäftigen und diese zu üben. Und vielen ist dabei unwohl, denn Grammatik wird oft mit unverständlichen Regeln, Pauken und großen Textmassen verbunden.

Viele dieser Menschen gehören zu den sogenannten „visuellen Lerntypen“, die besser lernen, wenn Lerninhalte visuell, also bildsprachlich, aufbereitet sind.

Visuelles Lernen leicht gemacht

Bilder – aber nicht nur Bilder, sondern auch Grafiken, Formen und Farbe helfen unserem Gehirn, Texte zu strukturieren und zu verstehen.

Dieses Prinzip macht sich dieses Buch zunutze und so können komplexe und „trockene“ Regeln übersichtlich und einfach dargestellt werden.

Dieses Übungsbuch ist dabei kein reines Bilderbuch, vielmehr unterstützt die Visualisierung den Text und hilft Ihnen so, sprachliche Inhalte besser zu verstehen und zu verarbeiten.

1 Bild sagt mehr als 1000 Worte

An diesem Sprichwort ist etwas Wahres dran, denn unser Gehirn kann Bilder und visuelle Darstellungen viel schneller aufnehmen als einen Text, der dieselben Inhalte wiedergibt. In der Tat benötigt es dafür nur den Bruchteil von Sekunden.

Werden Sie ruhig emotional ...

... denn an Dinge, für die Sie ein Gefühl entwickeln, erinnern Sie sich eine ganze Weile länger als an Dinge, die Sie „kaltlassen“.

Bilder und visuelle Darstellungen sind dabei bestens dazu geeignet, Emotionen zu vermitteln. Sie prägen sich leichter ein und sorgen für Motivation – die Grundlage für Ihren Lernerfolg!

Durch die Verknüpfung von grammatischen Inhalten und visuellen Darstellungen entsteht die Basis für entspanntes und positives Lernen.

PONS

Grammatik üben in Bildern
ENGLISCH

von
Tim Cater
und
Samuel Hemingway

PONS GmbH
Stuttgart

PONS

Grammatik üben in Bildern
ENGLISCH

von
Tim Cater
und
Samuel Hemingway

1. Auflage 2017

Projektleitung: Canan Eulenberger-Özdamar
Redaktion: Dominic Butler
Logoentwurf: Erwin Poell, Heidelberg
Logoüberarbeitung: Sabine Redlin, Ludwigsburg
Titelfotos: Apfel: Shutterstock/Dionisvera, Hund: Shutterstock/Brian Zanchi
Einbandgestaltung: Anne Helbich, Stuttgart
Layout: PONS GmbH, Stuttgart
Satz: tebitron gmbh, Gerlingen
Druck und Bindung: Publikum d.o.o.

Printed in the EU.
ISBN: 978-3-12-562872-4

So ist GRAMMATIK ÜBEN IN BILDERN aufgebaut:

In diesem Buch finden Sie in 17 Kapiteln **alle wichtigen Grammatikthemen der Niveaus A1 – B2** für das Englische.

1 HALLO & WILLKOMMEN!

Jedes Kapitel begrüßt Sie freundlich mit einem großformatigen Bild und stellt Ihnen kurz vor, **worum es in diesem Kapitel geht**.

2 Die Farben – AUGEN AUF UND DURCH!

In jedem Kapitel steht eine **Farbe für ein grammatisches Phänomen**, das im gesamten Kapitel ausschließlich durch diese Farbe gekennzeichnet wird.

Das Zusammenspiel von **Farbe, grafischen Gestaltungen** und **Bildern** erleichtert Ihnen das Lernen und Memorieren.

3 Die perfekte Ergänzung: GRAMMATIK IN BILDERN Englisch

Dieses Übungsbuch ist Teil der Reihe **VISUELLES LERNEN** und komplett analog aufgebaut zur Nachschlagegrammatik **GRAMMATIK IN BILDERN Englisch** (ISBN: 978-3-12-562685-0).

So können Sie zu jedem Kapitel des Übungsbuchs die entsprechenden Regeln im selben Kapitel der Grammatik nachschlagen. Umgekehrt finden Sie zu allen Regeln des Grammatikbuches Übungen in diesem Übungsbuch.

Das **Farbleitsystem** sorgt für schnelle Orientierung: Alle grammatischen Phänomene haben dieselben Farben in beiden Büchern.

Natürlich können aber beide Bücher **völlig unabhängig** voneinander verwendet werden.

Jeder kann Grammatik lernen – Sie müssen nur noch loslegen!

Wir wünschen Ihnen viel Erfolg & Freude dabei.

Ihre PONS-Redaktion

INHALT

If not now, when?

I wish
I could fly...

Call me!
Should
I call her?

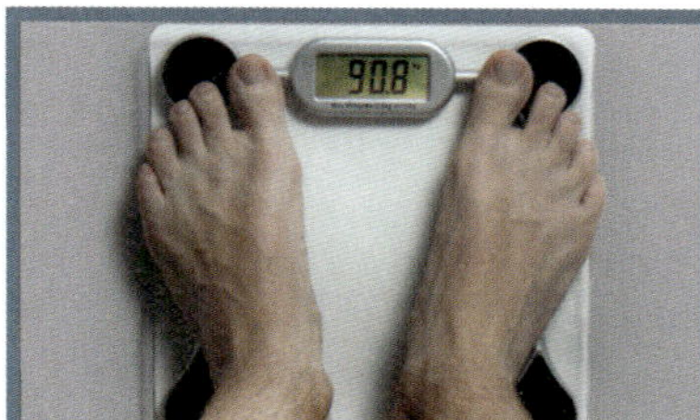

1 Der Artikel

Was sind Artikel und **wofür** brauche ich sie?

Welche Artikel gibt es im Englischen?

Und **wann** benutze ich welchen?

HE GAP

1. Bestimmter oder unbestimmter Artikel?

Entscheiden Sie, ob in den folgenden Fällen der bestimmte oder unbestimmte Artikel benötigt wird. Manchmal fällt der Artikel ganz weg!

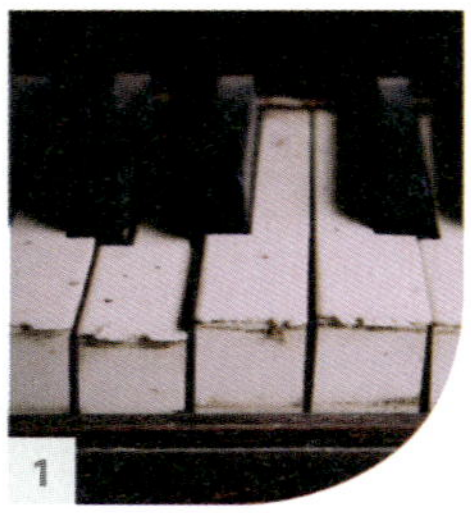

1

My sister plays ____ piano in a band. She's also ____ piano teacher.

2

And my brother is ____ famous rock star.

3

In the sky there are ____ million stars and ____ moon.

4

Patrick is ____ dreamer.

5

____ train will arrive in 2 minutes.

the

Den **bestimmten Artikel** verwendet man für näher bestimmte Dinge, aber z.B. auch für Familien- und Ländernamen, Regionen, öffentliche Einrichtungen oder bekannte Dinge. Der **unbestimmte Artikel** findet Verwendung bei nicht näher definierten Dingen oder auch bei der Bezeichnung von Berufen oder Nationalitäten. Bei unbestimmten Mengen wird oft **kein Artikel** verwendet.

6

Would you like ____ coffee for breakfast?

7

____ party was a great success!

a/an

8

Have you visited ____ London Eye?

9

Shall we have another match on ____ Saturday?

10

We went to ____ museum with ____ school.

2. *A* oder *an*?

Was sehen Sie auf den Bildern? Schreiben Sie die englische Bezeichnung unter das Foto und verbinden Sie es dann mit dem passenden Artikel.

1. ______________________

2 ______________________

3. ______________________

4. ______________________

5. ______________________

a

6. ______________________

7. ______________________

8. ______________________

9. ____________________

10. ____________________

11. ____________________

12. ____________________

an

13. ____________________

14. ____________________

15. ____________________

16. ____________________

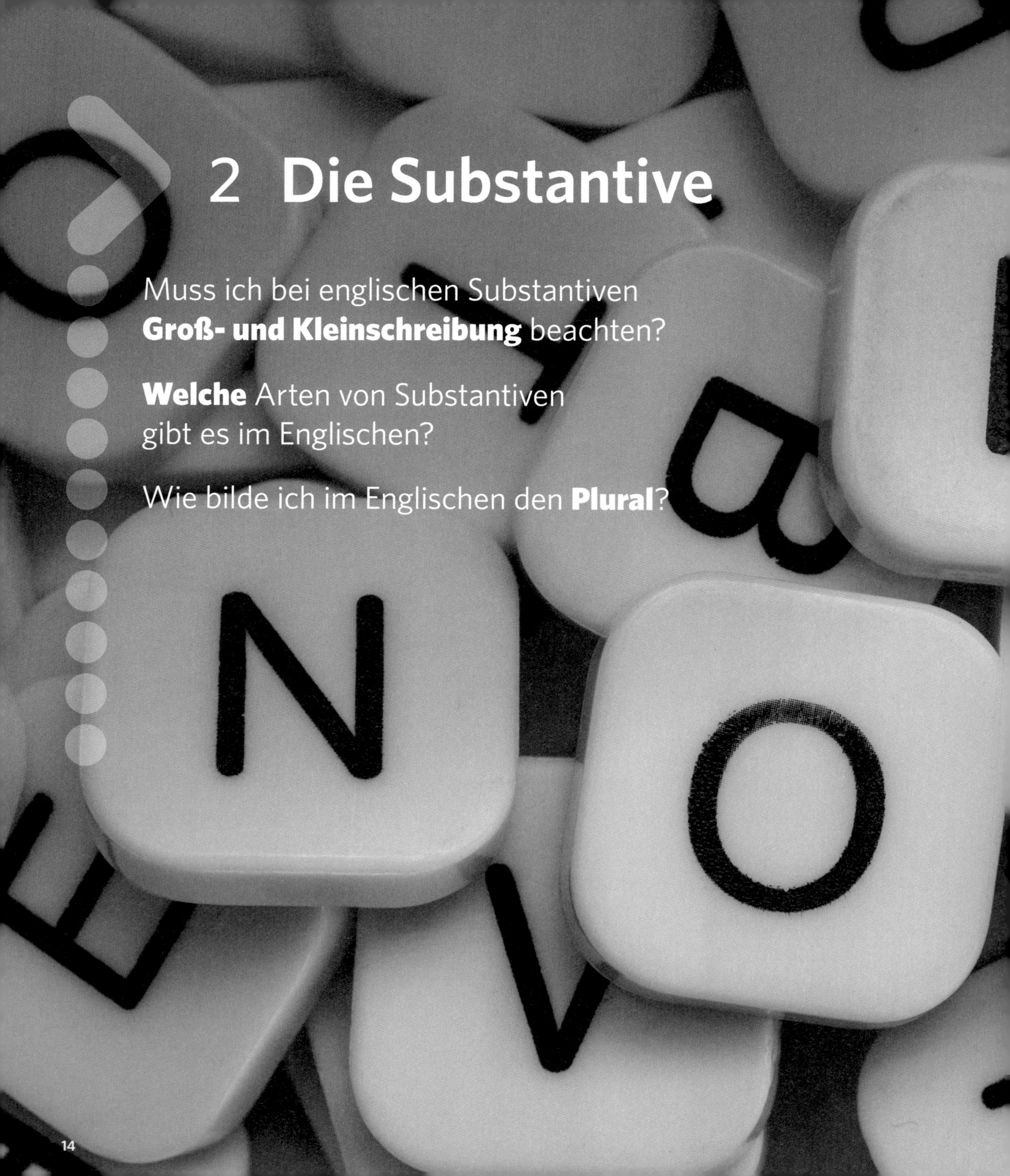

2 Die Substantive

Muss ich bei englischen Substantiven **Groß- und Kleinschreibung** beachten?

Welche Arten von Substantiven gibt es im Englischen?

Wie bilde ich im Englischen den **Plural**?

Y
U
N

1. Groß oder klein?

Ordnen Sie die Bildern den Sätzen zu und vervollständigen Sie die Sätze mit den passenden Wörtern. Entscheiden Sie, ob groß- oder kleingeschrieben werden muss.

1. ☐ Kate's getting married in ______________ .
2. ☐ I'm going to ______________ on business next month.
3. ☐ Are you going to the concert next ______________ ?
4. ☐ I'm flying to New York for ______________ next week.
5. ☐ Tom's new girlfriend is ______________ .
6. ☐ She's going to visit ______________ tomorrow.

2. Mr, Mrs und ein paar mehr

Welche Anrede oder welcher Titel passt hier?
Schreiben Sie die Abkürzung zum Bild.

Dr

Mr

1. ______________

2. ______________

3. ______________

Ms

Prof

Mrs

4. ______________

5. ______________

3. Eins, zwei, viele!

Schreiben Sie die Pluralformen der Wörter.

1. fox

1. ____________________

2. sandwich

2. ____________________

3. boy

3. ____________________

4. wolf

4. ____________________

5. strawberry

5. ____________________

6. glass

6. ____________________

4. Zählbar oder nicht?

Gehören diese Dinge zu den zählbaren oder nicht zählbaren Substantiven? Ordnen Sie sie zu und schreiben Sie die Dinge im Plural oder Singular auf.

ZÄHLBAR

UNZÄHLBAR

5. Nur Plural!

Vervollständigen Sie die Sätze mit den Substantiven in der korrekten Form.

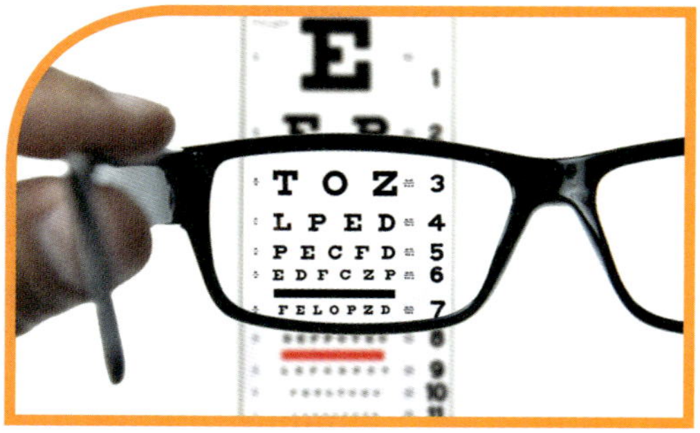

1. My brother wears ______ .

2. His jacket and ______ are very smart.

3. Please can I borrow the ______ ?

4. I need to buy a new pair of ______ .

5. She loves to shop for new ______ .

6. Be careful on the ______ !

6. Er, sie, es ...

Vervollständigen Sie die Sätze mit *he, she* oder *it*.

1. My girlfriend works very hard.
   ______'s a banker.
2. Is that your uncle?
   ______'s waving at us.
3. Do you like my new car?
   Have you seen ______?
4. My wife loves her job,
   but ______ works very long hours.
5. This phone is great.
   I'm going to buy ______.
6. Do you know his brother?
   ______'s an actor.

Merken Sie sich:
Bei *he, she, it* -
das *s* muss mit!

7. Was machen diese Leute?

Schauen Sie sich die Bilder und Wörter an. Bilden Sie dann Sätze mit *he* oder *she*, wie im Beispiel.

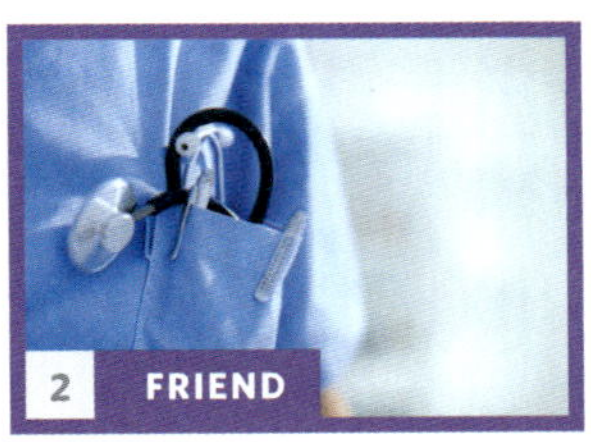

1. *Tom is my cousin. He is a photographer.*
2. *Jason is Tom's...*
3. *Here's my...*
4. *And this is Tom's...*

8. Der s-Genitiv

Wem gehören diese Dinge? Vervollständigen Sie die Sätze.

1. It's ________________ .

2. It's ________________ .

3. It's my ________________ .

4. It's ________________ .

5. They're the ________________ .

6. They're the ________________ .

9. Der of-Genitiv

Vervollständigen Sie die Sätze mit der korrekten Genitivform.

1. The school's name is Ashley Heath School.

The ______________________________ is Ashley Heath School.

2. Spain's tourist industry is growing.

The ______________________________ is growing.

3. London's history is very interesting.

The ______________________________ is very interesting.

4. The building's top floor is closed for renovation.

The ______________________________

is closed for renovation.

Achtung! Man benutzt den **of-Genitiv** um die Zugehörigkeit von Dingen oder Sachverhalten auszudrücken.

3 Die Pronomen

Was sind Pronomen?

Wofür werden sie verwendet?

Welche Pronomen gibt es im Englischen?

He did it!

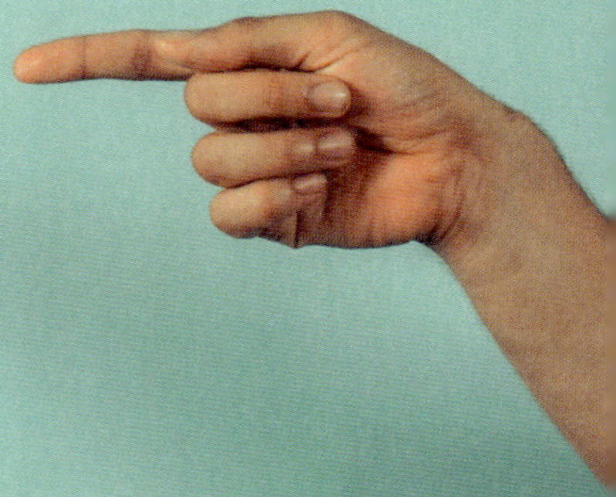

1. Jetzt wird's persönlich!

Vervollständigen Sie die Sätze mit den passenden Personalpronomen.
Entscheiden Sie dann, ob es sich um Subjekt- (SP) oder Objektpronomen (OP) handelt.

1. ________________ loves her new car.

SP ☐ OP ☐

2. She drives ________________ to work every day.

SP ☐ OP ☐

3. I saw Beth and Paul last week. Have you invited ________________ to the party?

SP ☐ OP ☐

4. Oh, no. Look at Paul. ________________ hates tennis.

SP ☐ OP ☐

5. Jon gave ________________ some money. I think she spent all of it!

SP ☐ OP ☐

6. His parents didn't enjoy the concert. ________________ hate loud music.

SP ☐ OP ☐

2. Besitzverhältnisse

Tragen Sie die passenden Possessivpronomen in die Lücken ein.
Die angegebenen deutschen Pronomen helfen Ihnen.

Possessivpronomen werden an Stelle eines Nomens verwendet:

Is that *your* coat? It's the same colour as mine.

1

My brother has broken ________ (sein) leg.

2

Can I borrow ________ (dein) camera, please?

3

I helped ________ (mein) brother with his training.

4

Don't forget to give Sally and David ________ (ihr) presents.

5

Francis is working on ________ (ihr) essay.

6

My car is small, but ________ (dein) is big.

7

Can I use your mobile? ________ (mein) is broken.

8

Did you remember to give them ________ (unser) phone number?

3. Reflexivpronomen

Können Sie das Kreuzworträtsel lösen? Tragen sie die richtigen Reflexivpronomen ein.

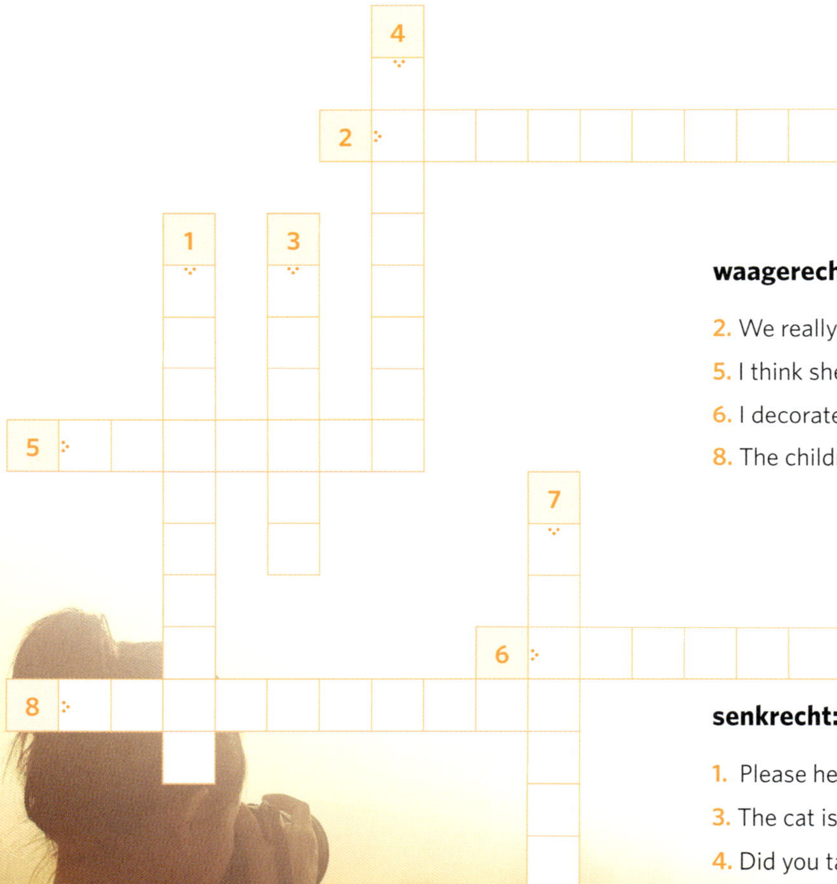

waagerecht:

2. We really enjoyed ... at the park.
5. I think she made it ... .
6. I decorated the room ... .
8. The children cleaned the room ... .

senkrecht:

1. Please help ... to some coffee.
3. The cat is cleaning ... .
4. Did you take the photo ... ?
7. He told me he cooked it ... .

4. Demonstrativformen

Schauen Sie sich die Fotos an und schreiben Sie Sätze mit *this, that, those* und *these*.

1. ____________ TV programme is so boring!

2. ____________ is his house.

3. ____________ are my friends.

4. ____________ are vegetables from our garden.

5. Allgemeine Personalpronomen

Füllen Sie die Lücken mit den Wörtern in den Kästchen.

they / people

you

one

he / she

1. ____________ must do what ____________ is told.

2. ____________ cannot always do what ____________ want.

3. ____________ can't always find what ____________ need in that shop.

4. If your child is thinking of a career in retail, ____________ or ____________ can get information from this website.

6. Indefinitpronomen

Ordnen Sie den Indefinitpronomen die richtige Definition zu.

____ **A** nichts von etwas

____ **B** wird in verneinten Sätzen anstelle von *some* verwendet

____ **C** eine unbestimmte Menge

____ **D** eins/keins von den beiden

Indefinitpronomen werden für nicht näher spezifizierte Personen, Dinge oder Orte verwendet.

____ E Individuen einer Gruppe

____ F beide, der eine und der andere

____ G die komplette Menge von etwas

____ H ersetzt ein bereits erwähntes zählbares Nomen

4 Die Präpositionen

Was sind Präpostionen?

Welche Präpostionen verwende ich für Zeit-, Orts- und Richtungsangaben?

Was muss ich beachten?

above
below

1. Was war wann?

Schauen Sie sich Simons Urlaubsfotos an und vervollständigen Sie die Sätze mit den passenden Präpositionen der Zeit.

1. This year, I decided to go on holiday ________ June.

2. My flight left the airport ________ 11.30.

on

at/around

during

in

3. ________ the evening I travelled by train to a small town.

4. I decided to relax ________ my first day.

5. Every day ________ breakfast I read my book.

6. Most evenings, I sat outside ________ sunset.

until

for

in

since

at

7. I usually had lunch ________ midday.

8. Next year, I want to go on holiday ________ two weeks.

9. ________ that lovely holiday, I've been thinkng about my next trip!

2. Wo und wohin?

Was machen die Katzen in diesen Bildern? Setzen Sie die passenden Präpositionen für Ortsangaben ein.

under — against — over — in — on — behind — in front of — by — next to

1. The cat is ____________ the deck chair.

2. The cat is hiding ____________ the the box.

3. The cat is sleeping ____________ the deck chair.

4. The cat is washing itself ____________ the fire.

5. The fish is jumping ____________ the cat.

6. The cat is ____________ the fish bowl.

7. The cat is leaning ____________ the dog.

8. The cat is ____________ the door.

9. The cat is ____________ Sarah.

3. Wo ist was?

Mia beschreibt das Zimmer ihrer kleinen Schwester.
Vervollständigen Sie die Sätze mit den passenden Ortspräpositionen.

on | in | under | next to | against | above | in front of

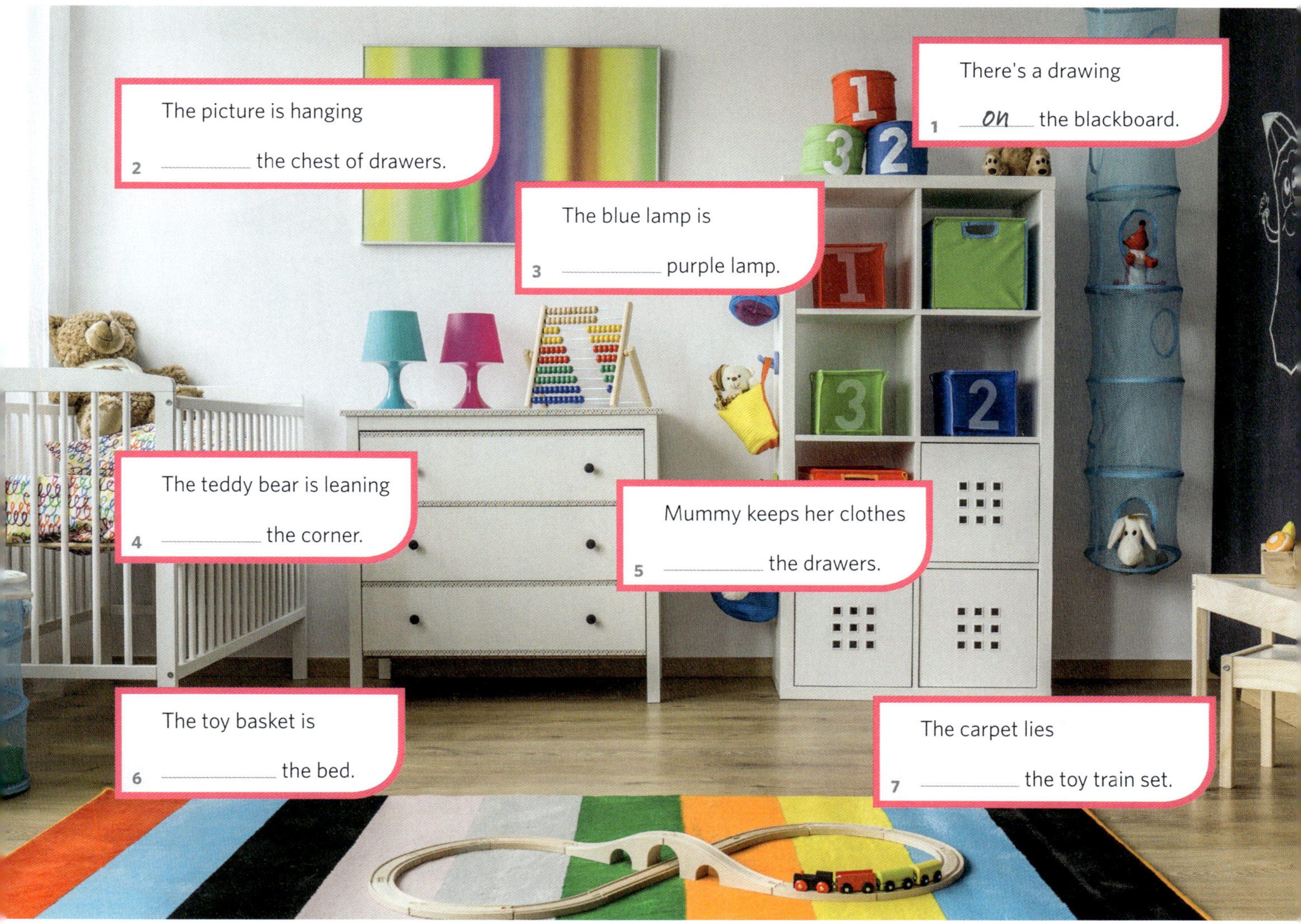

1 There's a drawing ___on___ the blackboard.

2 The picture is hanging ________ the chest of drawers.

3 The blue lamp is ________ purple lamp.

4 The teddy bear is leaning ________ the corner.

5 Mummy keeps her clothes ________ the drawers.

6 The toy basket is ________ the bed.

7 The carpet lies ________ the toy train set.

4. Schulstart!

Welche Richtungspräpositionen gehören in die Lücken? Tragen Sie sie ein.

1

The bus takes the kids _from_ their homes _to_ school.

2

They get ______ the bus and say good morning to the driver.

3

It drives ______ the street picking up kids on the way.

4

The bus drives ______ the bridge...

5

...and ______ a tunnel.

6

Finally, the kids get off the bus and go ______ school.

into

along

onto

through

over

~~from~~

~~to~~

5. Ein neuer Morgen

Der Schulbus ist wieder einmal unterwegs ... Nutzen Sie Zeit und füllen Sie die Lücken mit den passenden Präpositionen für Grund, Folge und Zweck.

to of for

1. The school bus was delayed because _of_ the traffic jam.
2. All the kids get to school on time thanks ____ the driver.
3. The cool kids always sit at the back ____ the bus.
4. Everyone is asleep on the bus in the morning...except ____ the driver.
5. School was closed on Wednesday due ____ the teachers' strike.
6. In spite ____ being late, Kim still managed to get the bus.

5 Die Adjektive

Was sind Adjektive?

Wofür benötige ich sie?

Wie bilde ich sie?

happy

sad

1. Adjektive

Ordnen Sie die Bildern zuerst den passenden Adjektiven in Box 1 zu.
Ordnen Sie dann die Begriffe ihren passenden Gegenteilen in Box 2 zu.

1

1 A happy
___ B delicious
___ C long
___ D hard/difficult
___ E hungry
___ F active
___ G tall
___ H old (object)
___ I old (person)

2

delicious / disgusting
________ / short
________ / full
________ / lazy
________ / sad
________ / easy
________ / short
________ / young
________ / new

2. Viele unterschiedliche Formen

Schauen Sie sich die Wörter in den Kästchen an. Mit der passenden Endung werden sie zu Adjektiven. Bilden Sie sie und schreiben Sie sie in die kleinen Kästchen zur passenden Endung.

care | season | expense | dead | fool | nation

adventure | comfort | danger | use | friend | cloud | act

child | wool | end | wind | accept | fame | culture

self | storm | reason | defense | heart | peace

-ful

careful

-al

-ous

-able

-ive

-ish

-less

-ly

-y

3. Eine Frage der Form

Wählen Sie das richtige Partizip *(present/past participle)* und füllen Sie die Lücken.

1 The ________ (sleeping/slept) child woke up when she heard the ________ (crying/cried) baby.

2 The ________ (boring/bored) girl looked out of the window at the ________ (pouring/poured) rain.

3 The ________ (losing/lost) dog walked through the city in the ________ (falling/fallen) snow.

4 The ________ (winning/won) team will receive a ________ (signing/signed) shirt.

4. Nationalitäten

Aus Nationalitäten lassen sich Partizipien ableiten, die dann als Adjektive verwendet werden. Finden Sie die richtigen Partizipien und schreiben Sie sie zu den Flaggen.

1. The English flag

2. The ____________ flag

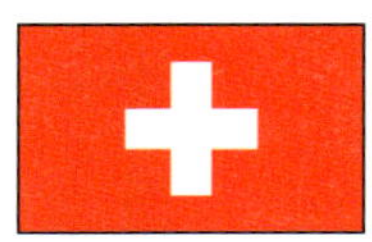

3. The ____________ flag

4. The ____________ flag

5. The ____________ flag

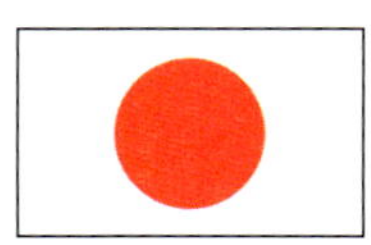

6. The ____________ flag

England

Switzerland

Japan

France

Thailand

America

5. Vergleiche

Auf der Tafel wurden aus Versehen einige Adjektive und ihre Steigerungsformen gelöscht. Tragen Sie sie wieder ein.

GRUNDFORM	KOMPARATIV	SUPERLATIV
tall		
	shorter	
		the biggest
thin		
		the largest
	nicer	
funny		
		the laziest
	prettier	
	more dangerous	
comfortable		
unregelmäßige Adjektive		
		the best
	worse	
		the furthest/ the farthest

6. Und noch mehr Vergleiche

Gut, dass Sie die Adjektive auf S. 45 eingefügt haben! Sie benötigen Sie, um die Lücken dieser Übung zu füllen. Bilden Sie Vergleiche.

The Burj Khalifa is *the* *tallest* building in the world.

1

The high road is ______ than the low road.

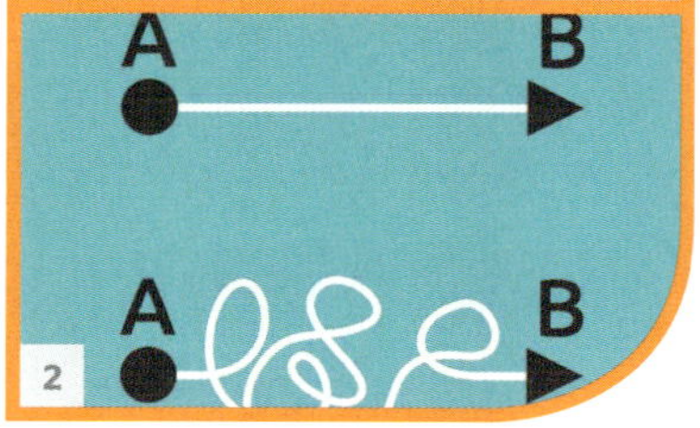

2

Goliath was much ______ than David thought.

3

The man on the right looks ______ than the one on the left.

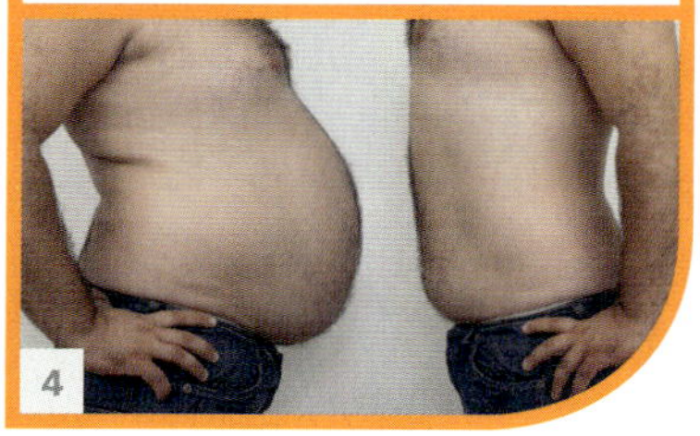

4

This must be ______ ______ beach in the world.

5

That's ______ ______ thing I've heard all week.

6

Sometimes I think my dog is ______ than other dogs.

7

These are ______ ______ flowers in my garden.

8

The deathstalker is one of ______ ______ animals on the planet.

9

7. Groß und giftig!

Hier einige der größten und giftigsten Tiere der Welt! Aber sie sind nicht alle gleich groß oder gefährlich. Vergleichen Sie sie miteinander und benutzen Sie *(not) as...as, than* oder den Superlativ.

1. The giraffe is bigger than the brown bear.

The brown bear is _not as big as_ the giraffe.

2. The colossal squid is ______ ______ the blue whale.

The colossal squid is not as big as the blue whale.

3. The African elephant is bigger than the giraffe.

The giraffe ____________________

4. A blue whale's tongue weighs the same as a car.

A blue whale's tongue is ____________________ a car.

5. The box jellyfish is ____ ______ ________ animal.

All the other animals are not as poisonous as the box jellyfish.

6. The octopus is less poisonous than the snail.

The octopus is ____________________

7. The king cobra is a little less dangerous than the jellyfish.

The jellyfish is nearly ____________________ the king cobra.

8. Eine Frage der Position

Beschreiben Sie die Bilder, indem Sie das passende Nomen und Adjektiv finden.

1. *a delicious burger*

6. ______

2. ______

warm, woolly	statue
famous, old	watch
active, young	jumper
delicious	woman
cold, windy	burger
expensive	day

5. ______

3. ______

4. ______

9. Der schönste Tag ...

Diese Hochzeit bleibt in Erinnerung! Vervollständigen Sie den Text.
Die Hinweise in den kleinen Kästchen helfen Ihnen.

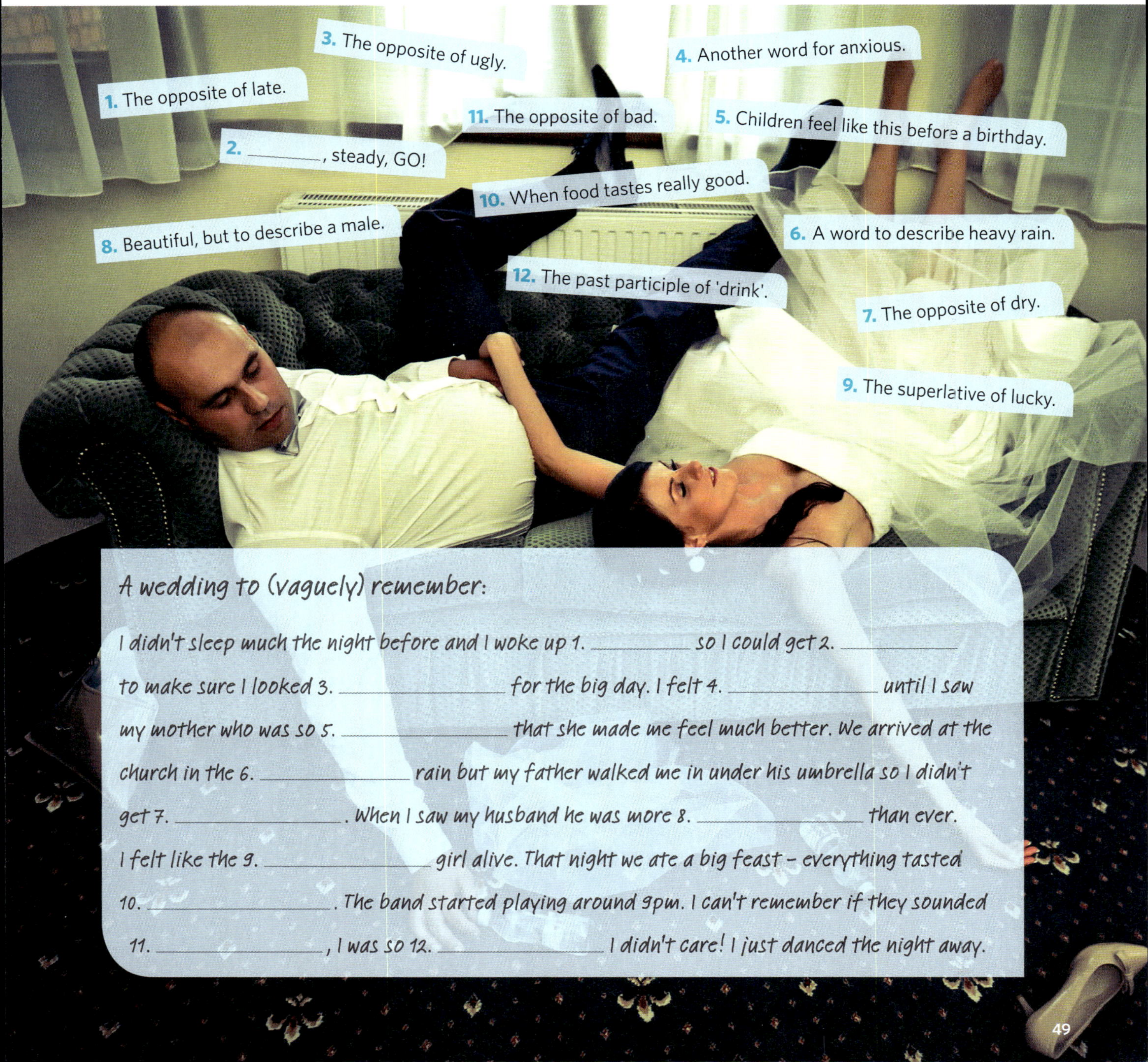

1. The opposite of late.
2. ________, steady, GO!
3. The opposite of ugly.
4. Another word for anxious.
5. Children feel like this before a birthday.
6. A word to describe heavy rain.
7. The opposite of dry.
8. Beautiful, but to describe a male.
9. The superlative of lucky.
10. When food tastes really good.
11. The opposite of bad.
12. The past participle of 'drink'.

A wedding to (vaguely) remember:

I didn't sleep much the night before and I woke up 1. ________ so I could get 2. ________ to make sure I looked 3. ________ for the big day. I felt 4. ________ until I saw my mother who was so 5. ________ that she made me feel much better. We arrived at the church in the 6. ________ rain but my father walked me in under his umbrella so I didn't get 7. ________. When I saw my husband he was more 8. ________ than ever. I felt like the 9. ________ girl alive. That night we ate a big feast – everything tasted 10. ________. The band started playing around 9pm. I can't remember if they sounded 11. ________, I was so 12. ________ I didn't care! I just danced the night away.

6 Die Adverbien

Was ist der **Unterschied** zwischen einem Adjektiv und einem Adverb?

Wofür benötige ich Adverbien?

Wie **bilde** ich sie?

She waited **patiently** for her husband.

1. Adjektive und Adverbien

Unterstreichen Sie zuerst alle Adjektive (pink) und alle Adverbien (orange) in den durcheinandergeratenen Sätzen. Schreiben Sie dann die Sätze in der korrekten Form auf.

1. ______________________________

2. ______________________________

3. ______________________________

4. ______________________________

5. ______________________________

2. Aus Adjektiv wird Adverb!

Wandeln Sie die Adjektive in Adverbien um, die auf *-ly* enden.

1. quiet		**2.** normal		**3.** careful	
4. happy		**5.** probable		**6.** terrible	

3. Adjektiv oder Adverb?

Welche der fett gedruckten Wörter sind Adjektive und welche Adverbien? Tragen Sie sie in das korrekte Kästchen ein.

			Adjektiv	Adverb
1		She closed the **back** door and went **left** down the steet.		
2		I was in such a **deep** sleep that I woke up **late**.		
3	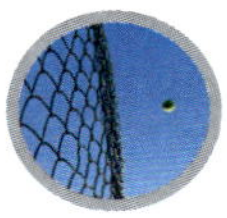	He hit the ball **hard**, and it flew over the **high** fence.		
4	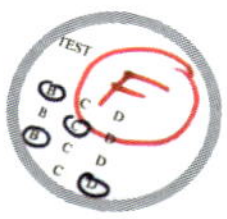	The test was really **hard** and he got most of the answers **wrong**.		
5		He can **hardly** drive, but that didn't stop him from buying a **fast** car.		
6		Mmmm, what a **lovely** smell! It must be **nearly** dinner time!		

4. Steigerung der Adverbien

Verwenden Sie die Steigerungen mit *-er/-erst* und *more/most*, um die folgenden Adverbien zu steigern. Achten Sie auf die unregelmäßigen Formen!

1. She sings...	beautifully 	______ 	______ 
2. He drinks...	quickly 	______ 	______ 
3. She arrived...	late 	______ 	______ 
4. He climbed...	high 	______ 	______ 
5. That team are playing...	well 1:0	______ 3:0	______ 4:0
6. I write...	badly 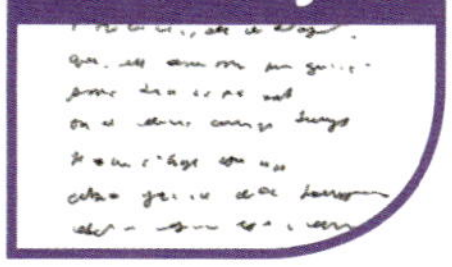	______ 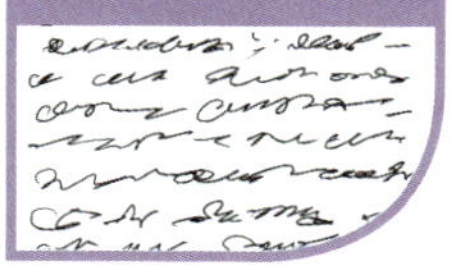	______ 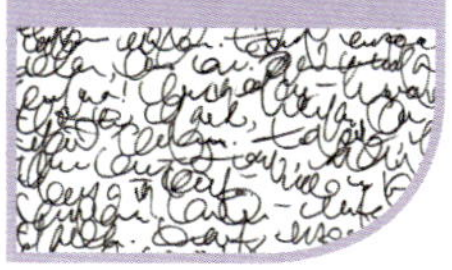

5. Es geht immer schlimmer?

In England gibt es wirklich schlechte Autofahrer. Schauen Sie sich die Top-5 der größten Verkehrssünder an und vervollständigen Sie anschließend die Lücken, indem Sie Vergleiche bilden.

The UK's Worst Drivers

Top 5

Most points scored on a driving test.

1. Oxford
2. Liverpool
3. Basildon
4. Wigan
5. Burnley

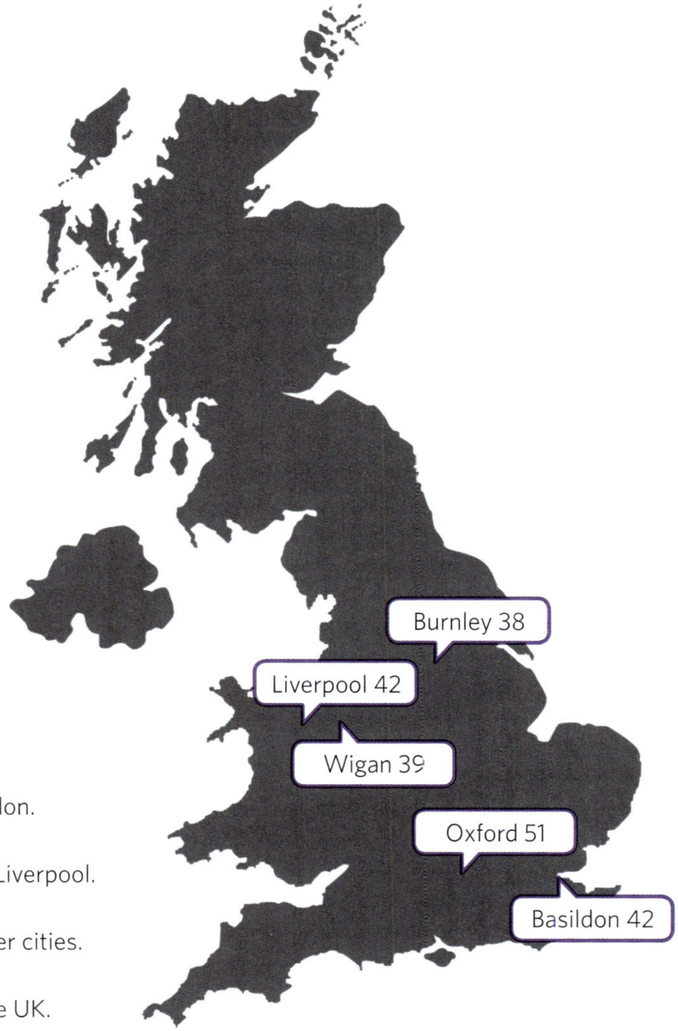

1. People in Oxford drive the ______ in the UK.
2. People in Liverpool drive ___ badly ___ people in Basildon.
3. People in Wigan drive ____ carefully than people in Liverpool.
4. People in Burnley drive _____ than people in the other cities.
5. People in Oxford don't drive ___ well ___ the rest of the UK.

6. Die Stellung des Adverbs

Finden Sie die Adverbien in der Wortspirale und tragen Sie sie in die Kästchen ein. Verwenden Sie diese dann, um die Lücken in den folgenden Sätzen zu vervollständigen.

1. ______ 2. ______ 3. ______

4. ______ 5. ______ 6. ______

7. ______ 8. ______ 9. ______

I hate baking. I bake **A** ______ .

B I ______ bake. Except for Sundays, when my mother-in-law comes round for tea.

My mother-in-law is a **C** ______ good cook, of course. All the cakes she makes are just perfect.

She **D** ________ criticises my attempts.

"**E** ________ is not your day, is it dear?" she says.

One Sunday, after dancing **F** ________ all night and getting **G** ________ any sleep, I decided to cheat.

I walked **H** ________ down to the shop and bought the nicest cake they had.

"Mmm, delicious! Your cakes don't **I** ________ taste this good!"

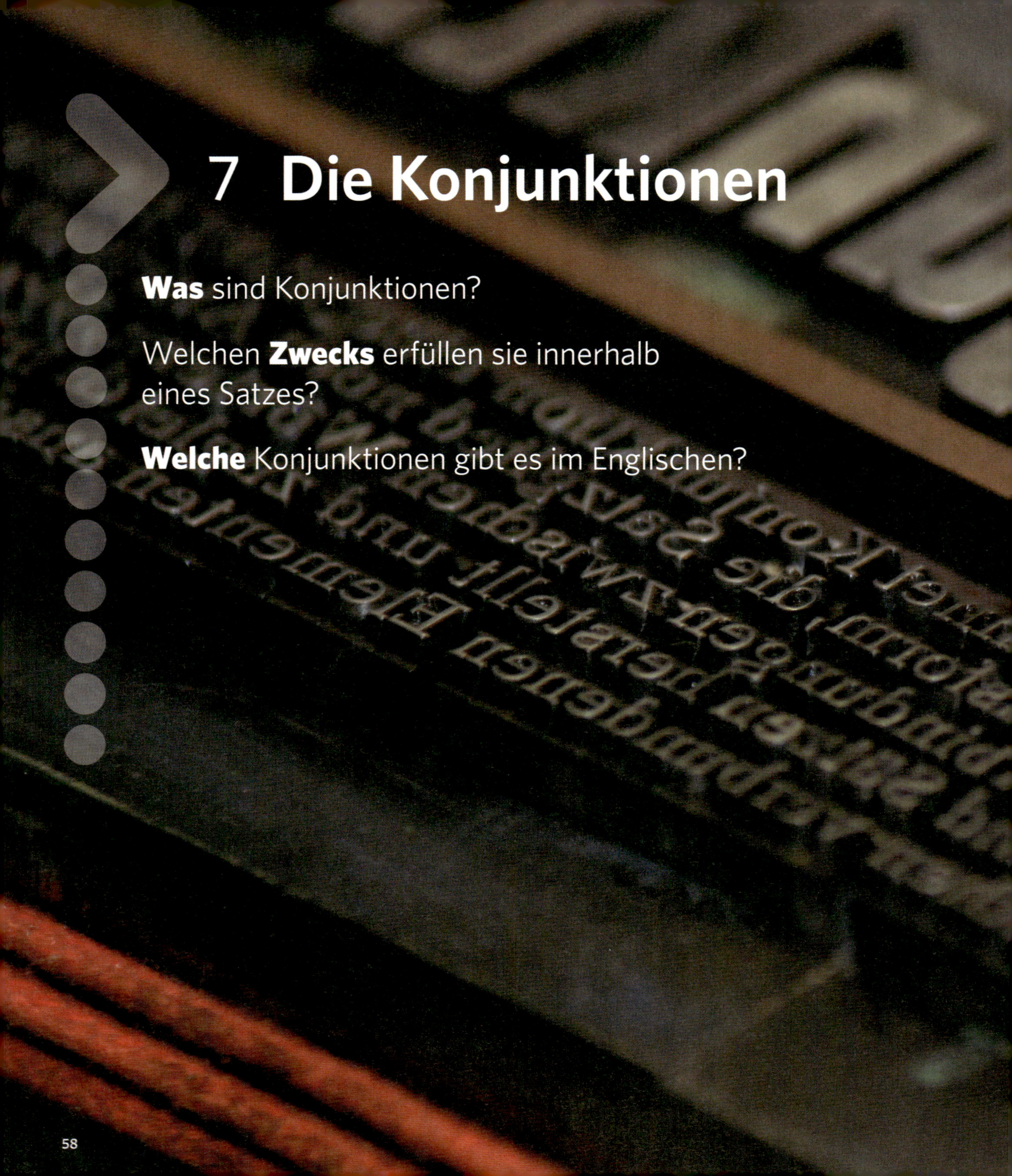

7 Die Konjunktionen

Was sind Konjunktionen?

Welchen **Zwecks** erfüllen sie innerhalb eines Satzes?

Welche Konjunktionen gibt es im Englischen?

Viele unterschiedliche Konjunktionen

Lesen Sie die Informationen über die Autos und befüllen Sie die Lücken. Achtung: es gibt nebenordnende und unterordnende Konjunktionen und solche, die getrennt im Satz stehen.

Review: Electric Car

The electric car is **1.** ________ smooth and surprisingly fast.

2. ________ it takes a long time to charge, it's very eco-friendly

3. ________ you won't feel bad about damaging the environment.

Be warned, you can only drive **4.** ________ the charge runs out!

both

until

although

so

so that

because

neither

and

but

Review: Off-Road Vehicle

The off-road vehicle is **5.** ________ cheap nor eco-friendly, **6.** ________ it is awesome! It has amazing power **7.** ________ technology, **8.** ________ you can navigate your way through a jungle. Don't worry, no gorillas will bother you **9.** ________ this is one of the strongest and safest cars you can buy.

8 Die Verben

Was sind Verben und **was** drücken sie in einem Satz aus?

Welche **Arten** von Verben gibt es im Englischen?

VERB
verb

1. Es gibt viel zu tun!

Lieben, schlafen essen ... diese Dinge sind elementar. Ebenso wichtig ist es zu wissen, ob Verben regelmäßig oder unregelmäßig sind - abhängig davon müssen Sie nämlich auf die Vergangenheitsformen achten. Entscheiden Sie, wie es bei den folgenden Verben aussieht und tragen Sie sie in die richtige Tabelle ein.

REGELMÄSSIGE VERBEN (PARTIZIP AUF *-ED*)
love

UNREGELMÄSSIGE VERBEN (PARTIZIP AUF *-ED*)	PAST SIMPLE	PAST PARTICIPLE
learn	learnt	learnt

2. Mit oder ohne?

Manche Verben benötigen ein Objekt, damit der Satz sinnvoll ist (transitiv), mache nicht (intransitiv) und manche beziehen sich auf das Subjekt (reflexiv). Schauen Sie sich die Sätze in den Eiswürfeln an und verbinden Sie sie mit dem richtigen Glas.

TRANSITIV

INTRANSITIV

REFLEXIV

3. Die Liebe kommt, die Liebe geht

Lesen Sie, wie die Beziehung dieses Paares früher war und heute ist. Füllen Sie die Lücken mit der korrekten Form des Hilfsverbs *be*. Verwenden Sie, wenn möglich, Kurzformen.

	In the past...	Now...
1	I **was** lonely until I found you.	I ______ wishing I had more time for myself.
2	You ______ the man of my dreams.	You ______ my worst nightmare.
3	He ______ my Romeo.	He ______ my couch potato.
4	We ______ perfect together.	We ______ perfectly happy to be apart.

4. Neue Bekanntschaften

Hier fehlt etwas – das Hilfsverb! Setzen Sie die korrekte Form von *be* (1. – 3.) oder *have* (4. – 6.) in die passende Lücke. Achten Sie auf die Zeiten und verwenden Sie, wenn möglich, Kurzformen.

present progressive

1. ____ She ____ meeting ____ new ____ people.

2. ____ she ____ forgetting ____ about ____ him ____?

simple present passive

3. ____ She ____ kissed ____ by ____ a ____ stranger.

present perfect

4. ____ She ____ left ____ her ____ old ____ life ____ behind.

5. ____ They ____ seen ____ each ____ other ____ since.

past perfect

6. ____ What ____ if ____ he ____ made ____ more ____ effort?

5. Großes Durcheinander

Hier stimmt gar nichts mehr! Bringen Sie die Sätze in die richtige Reihenfolge und befüllen Sie die leeren Kästchen mit der korrekten Form des Vollverbs *do*. Achten Sie auf die Zeiten.

1 bed | the | comfortable | feel | ____ | ?

____

2 sleep | I | ____ | well. | No,

____

3 eggs | you | like | ? | ____

____

4 eat | products. | I | dairy | ____

____

doesn't

didn't

do

does

did

don't

6. Noch mehr Durcheinander

Gehen Sie genauso vor wie in Übung 5. Verwenden Sie diesmal die korrekten Formen des Vollverbs *will* – auch hier mit Kurzformen, wenn möglich.

1 I | get up | ___ | soon.

____

2 The | last | day | forever. | ___

____

3 ___ | breakfast in bed | me | ? | you | make

____

will

won't

4 ___ | lunch | I | you | make | in bed!

____

7. So viele Verbote!

Im Klassenzimmer herrschen strikte Regeln. Was darf oder soll man und was nicht? Lesen Sie die Regeln auf der Pinnwand und unterstreichen Sie die Modalverben. Entscheiden Sie dann, ob die untenstehenden Aussagen richtig oder falsch sind.

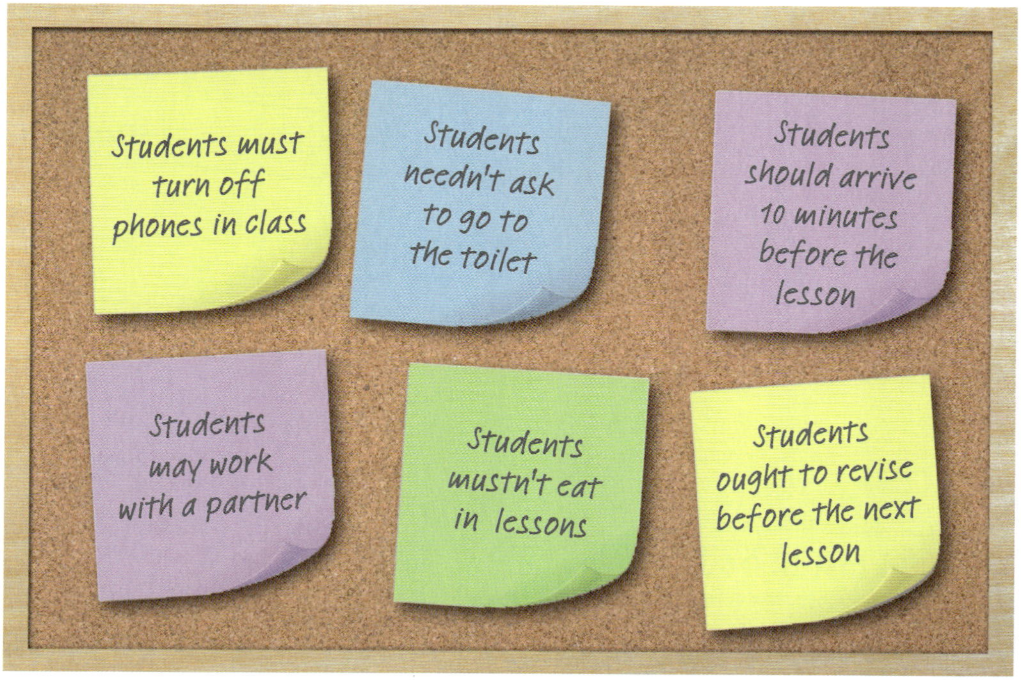

1. Students have to turn off their phones.
TRUE ☐ **FALSE** ☐

2. Students should ask to go to the toilet.
TRUE ☐ **FALSE** ☐

3. Students must arrive 10 minutes before class.
TRUE ☐ **FALSE** ☐

4. Students are allowed to work with a partner.
TRUE ☐ **FALSE** ☐

5. Students are supposed to eat in lessons.
TRUE ☐ **FALSE** ☐

6. Students are supposed to revise before the next lesson.
TRUE ☐ **FALSE** ☐

8. Vorschlagen oder befehlen

Modalverben helfen Bitten und Befehle zu formulieren und dabei höflich zu bleiben. In diesem Klassenzimmer wird viel gefragt. Unterstreichen Sie die Modalverben in den Sprechblasen und ordnen Sie die Sätze der passenden Funktion zu. Tragen Sie dazu die Nummern in das passende Kästchen unten ein.

9. Ein Verb, viele Möglichkeiten

Phrasal Verbs sind feste Verbindungen von Verben mit Präpositionen. Sie haben dadurch eigene Bedeutungen, die sich aus dem Verb allein nicht ableiten lassen. Im Wortgitter sind weitere 5 Präpositionen versteckt, durch die das Verb *look* eine jeweils andere Bedeutung bekommt. Finden Sie alle? Und können Sie auch die Übersetzung dazuschreiben?

d	a	g	e	t	r	m	n	p	z
m	f	o	r	w	a	r	d	t	o
a	e	e	w	m	f	g	r	e	m
g	f	s	a	i	t	l	l	o	h
g	r	o	h	n	e	i	a	g	s
i	o	i	r	h	r	o	u	k	s
o	d	m	n	r	s	o	b	e	i
r	a	t	u	e	r	e	e	t	m
e	r	f	i	h	t	t	i	m	o
a	m	i	t	i	m	o	h	u	p

1. to look after

sich um ...

2. to look ___ to

3. to look ___

4. to look ___

5. to look ___

6. to look ___

10. Vorschlagen oder befehlen

Verwenden Sie die *Phrasal Verbs* aus Übung 9, um die Lücken in den untenstehenden Sätzen zu füllen.

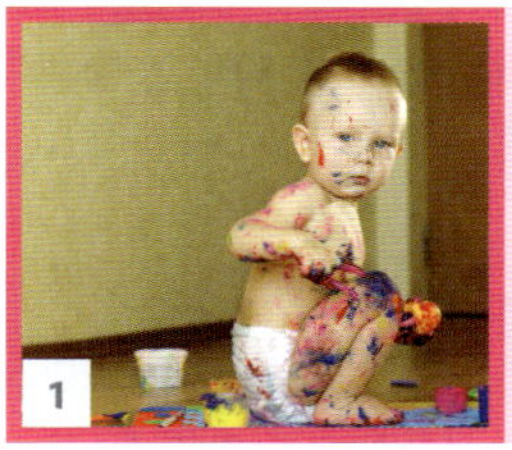

1 "The babysitter said she would look after the kids this evening, so we can go out!"

2 "Great! I ____ ____ ____ having a drink!"

3 "We should go – ____ ____ the time!"

4 "I can't find my wallet, please help me ____ ____ it."

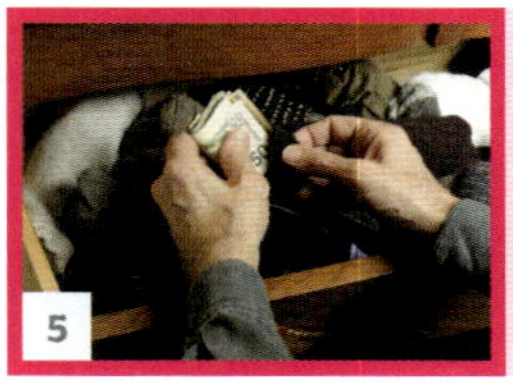

5 "Why don't you ____ ____ your sock drawer?"

6 "What's the restaurant called?" "I don't know ____ it ____ on your phone!"

11. Aufgepasst!

Den Imperativ verwenden Sie, um Befehle, Aufforderungen, Wünsche, Bitten oder Ratschläge zu formulieren. In der folgenden Unterhaltung zwischen dem abenteuerlustigen Colin und seinem besorgten Vater können Sie gleich einige Formen anwenden. Füllen Sie die Lücken mit den passenden Formen. Die Verwendung von *please* macht Aussagen höflicher. Und wer hat was gesagt? Verbinden Sie die Aussagen mit Vater oder Sohn.

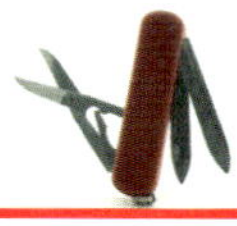

1. ______ careful, knives are sharp!

2. ______ hunt a rabbit!

3. ______ touch the fire!

Don't	Let's not
please	Help
Let's	Be
please	Help

5. ______ ______ ever go back home!

4. ______ me carry these safety ropes, ______.

6. ______ me find my bow and arrow, ______.

12. Aus Aktiv wird Passiv

Das Passiv wird verwendet, wenn nicht die handelnde Person, sondern die Handlung selbst im Vordergrund stehen soll. Setzen Sie die folgenden Sätze ins Passiv. Achten Sie auf die Zeiten.

present simple

past simple

Modalverb

Mr Sprinkles owns the cake factory.

Mr Sprinkles built the factory in 1991.

Everyone in town can smell the cakes.

1. The cake factory is owned by Mr Sprinkles.

2. ______________________________

3. ______________________________

The factory produces 11,000 cakes a day.

Mr Sprinkles invented a secret recipe for cupcakes.

No one must be given the secret recipe.

4. ______________________________

5. ______________________________

6. ______________________________

13. Rasante Abfahrt

Eine tolle Sache sind -*ing*-Formen! Mit ihnen können Sie im Handumdrehen aus einem Verb ein Substantiv zaubern. Einfach Grundform des Verbs + -*ing* und fertig ist die *ing*-Form, auch *gerund* genannt. Bilden Sie hier und auf der nächsten Seite die passenden Formen.

1. My family look forward to ______ skiing every winter.

2. My brother and I practise ______.

jump

feel

hit

3. We're getting good at ______ too!

slalom

go

4. Dad tries to avoid ______ trees...

5. and Mum always complains about ______ cold.

6. I think she just enjoys ______ the hotel spa.

7. Dad is considering ______ this year.

8. But I can't imagine him ______ cool on the slopes.

snowboard relax

9. Parents should stick to what they do best - ______

use look

14. Was für ein Mann!

Sue hat klare Erwartungen an Tom. Bilden Sie Sätze wie im Beispiel und verwenden Sie die *-ing*-Form oder den Infinitiv, je nachdem was das Verb erfordert.

Tom
Sue

keeps
wants
suggests
imagines
agrees
expects

+ infinitive
+ gerund

1 *Tom keeps bringing* (bring) Sue flowers.

2 ______________ (take) Sue on a date.

3 ______________ (go) for dinner.

4 ______________ (be) treated like a princess.

5 ______________ (date) him.

6 him ______________ (pay)!

15. Ein kleiner aber feiner Unterschied

Manche Verben verändern ihre Bedeutung, je nachdem, ob nach ihnen eine *-ing*-Form oder ein Infinitiv folgt. In dieser Aufgabe sehen Sie einige der wichtigsten dieser Verben. Verbinden Sie die Sätze mit den richtigen Beschreibungen.

stop

1 She stopped to drink a cocktail.

2 She stopped drinking her cocktail.

try

3 He tried to eat the oyster, but he couldn't.

4 He tried eating oysters and loved them.

remember

5 She remembered texting him back.

6 She remembered to text him back.

forget

7 He forgot to meet her at the restaurant.

8 He'll never forget meeting her.

A To attempt something difficult.

B To stop one activity and start another.

C To experiment with something to see if you like it.

D To remember an action that happened in the past.

E To stop an activity.

F To forget to do an activity.

G To forget an activity in the past (usually used with 'never').

H To remember something and then do it.

9 Die Zeiten

Welche Zeiten gibt es im Englischen?

Wie bilde ich sie?

Wann benutze ich welche?

Und **was** drücke ich mit der jeweiligen Zeit aus?

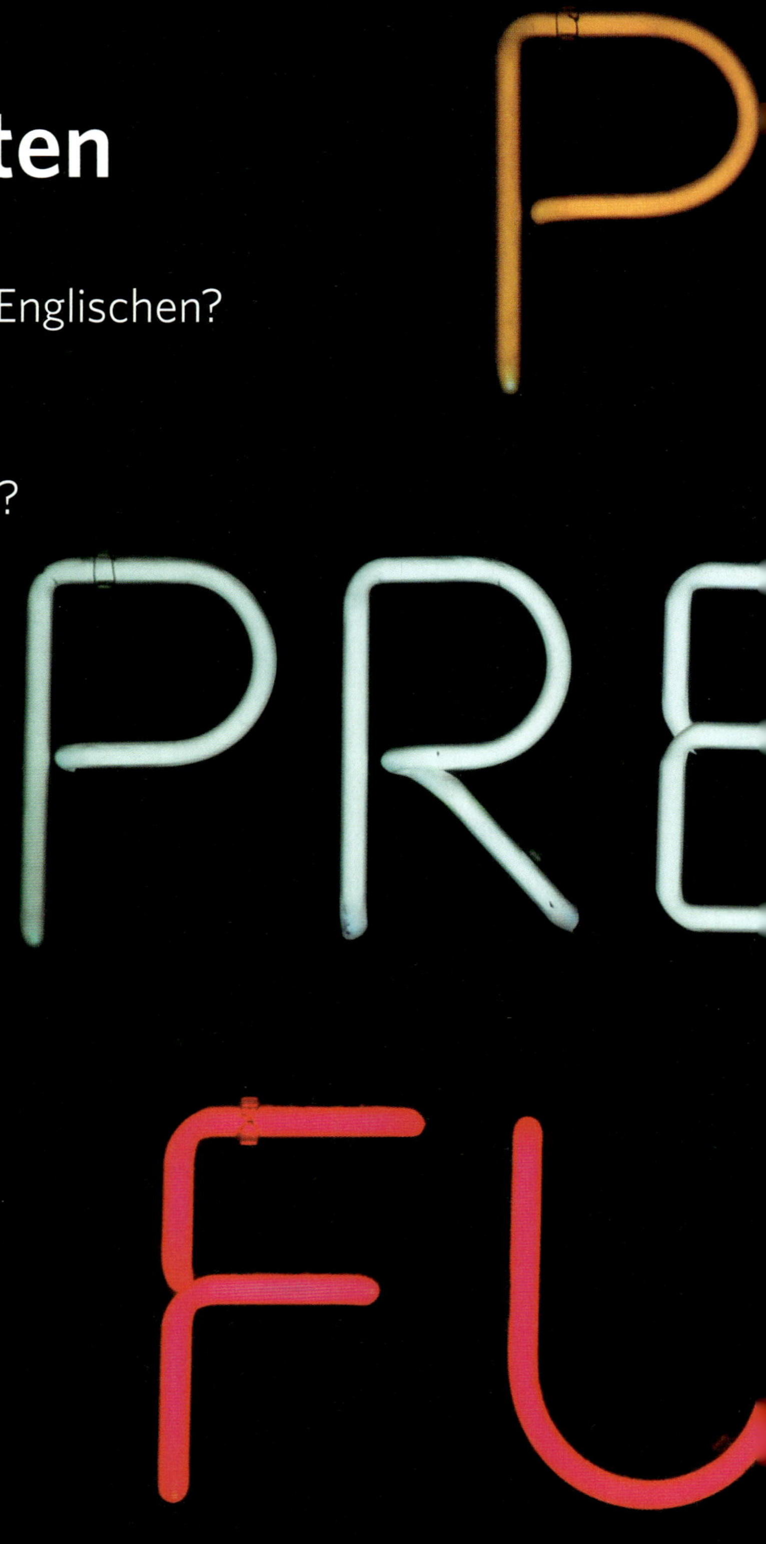

AST
SENT
TURE

1. Jahr für Jahr

Lesen Sie den Artikel über den nimmermüden Tony. Die fett markierten Verben sind Beispiele für jede der 12 Zeiten im Englischen. Schreiben Sie sie in die Tabelle auf der rechten Seite zu der richtgen Zeitform.

Time to take a break?

TONY HILL is a 78 year old runner from Birmingham, UK. **He has competed** three times for Great Britain in the Olympics. **He has been running** a mile every day for over 52 years! Now, **he is thinking** about taking a day off for the first time.

Last week **Tony had been running** his usual mile when he felt a problem. "After 400 metres **my heart was hurting**," he said. "Before that day **I had not experienced** any pain when running." Tony is very famous in the running scene. **He broke** the record for the London Marathon in 1970.

If Tony keeps running, by 2020 **he will have been running** everyday for 55 years, and **he will have set** a new world record!

"**I will run** for as long as I can," says Tony. "I hope **I will be running** when I'm 100!"

"I hope I will be running when I'm 100!"

PRESENT

1. *Tony Hill is…* ______	PRESENT SIMPLE
2. ______	PRESENT PROGRESSIVE
3. ______	PRESENT PERFECT
4. ______	PRESENT PERFECT PROGRESSIVE

PAST

5. ______	PAST SIMPLE
6. ______	PAST PROGRESSIVE
7. ______	PAST PERFECT
8. ______	PAST PERFECT PROGRESSIVE

FUTURE

9. ______	FUTURE SIMPLE
10. ______	FUTURE PROGRESSIVE
11. ______	FUTURE PERFECT
12. ______	FUTURE PERFECT PROGRESSIVE

10 Die Vergangenheit

Welche **Unterschiede** gibt es bei den Vergangenheitsformen des Englischen?

Wann verwende ich **welche** Form?

Was muss ich dabei beachten?

1. Aus und vorbei – das *past simple*

Mit dem *past simple* geben Sie im Englischen abgeschlossene Handlungen in der Vergangenheit wieder. Bilden Sie aus den regelmäßigen Verben, die Sie auf den Fotos sehen, das *past simple* auf *-ed*.

2. Eine Frage der Aussprache

Die regelmäßigen *past simple*-Formen enden zwar alle auf *-ed*, man spricht die Endung aber unterschiedlich aus – abhängig davon, wie die Grundform des Verbs endet. Tragen Sie die Verben aus Übung 1 in das passende Feld ein. Sollten Sie sich nicht mehr erinnern, liefert Ihnen die Box rechts unten auf dem Kopf einen Tipp!

[d]	[t]	[id]

Steht in der Grundform…
… Vokal + stimmhafter Konsonant = [d] ❯ (lov**ed**)
… stimmloser Konsonant = [t] ❯ (ask**ed**)
… d oder t = [id] (want**ed**) [id]

3. Jetzt wird es unregelmäßig

Schauen Sie sich die Bilder an. Was machen die Menschen? Schreiben Sie die *past simple*-Formen dieser unregelmäßigen Verben dazu. Manchmal ist mehr als eine Lösung möglich.

see · catch · teach · forget · go · learn · drink · bake · read · hear · learn · ~~buy~~

1 

buy
bought

2 

3 

4 

5 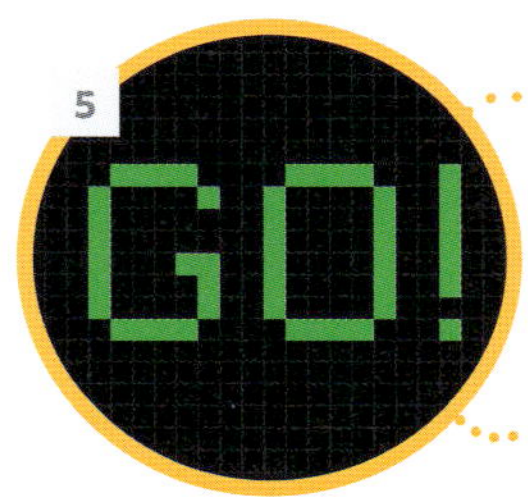

6 

7 

8 

9 

10 

4. *Did oder didn't?*

Bei Fragen oder Verneinungen verwenden Sie im *past simple* die Hilfsverben *did* oder *didn't*. Achtung! Nach *didn't* folgt die Grundform und nicht das *past simple*. Können Sie den folgenden Dialog vervollständigen? Verwenden Sie Kurzantworten.

1 ______ you watch Game Of Thrones last night?

2 No, I ______ .

3 ______ you forget?

4 Yes, I ______ .

5 You ______ miss anything. It was boring!

5. Klare Signale

Wie bei den Zeiten der Gegenwart helfen Ihnen auch bei den Zeiten der Vergangenheit einige Signalwörter, sich für die richtige Zeitform zu entscheiden. Hier sehen Sie einige Wörter, die auf das *past simple* schließen lassen. Setzen Sie sie in die richtigen Lücken.

when I was a student | a long time ago | last summer | when I was a little boy | yesterday | 5 minutes ago

 1	My mum read me fairytales every night ______ .	 2	______ I drank much more than I drink now.
 3	Where did my donkey go? It was here ______ .	 4	I had English lessons ______ when I was in high school.
 5	What did you do ______ ? I tried to make some cupcakes, but they were a disaster!	 6	Did you have a good holiday? Yes, but ______ was better.

6. Wer tat wann was?

Die Vergangenheit kann auch mit dem *past progressive* wiedergegeben werden, z.B. dann, wenn man sagen möchte, womit jemand zu einer bestimmten Zeit beschäftigt war. Erinnern Sie sich an die Bildung der Form? Ganz einfach: *was/were* + *-ing*-Form! Bilden Sie Sätze wie im Beispiel.

1. What was Nina doing at 17.00? *She was walking her dog on the beach.*
2. What was Rosie doing at 13.00?
3. What was Simon doing at 9.00?
4. What was Rosie doing at 17.00?
5. What was Rosie doing at 9.00?
6. What was/wasn't Simon doing at 13.00?
7. What was Simon doing at 17.00?
8. What was Nina doing at 13.00?
9. What was Nina eating at 9.00

7. Spaß im Schnee

Lesen Sie die Geschichte und verwenden Sie das *past progressive* um die Lücken zu füllen. Entscheiden Sie anschließend, welcher Funktion sich die Aussagen zuordnen lassen.

snow
walk

FUNKTION: Beschreibung der Szene und Hintergrundhandlungen

1. It was snowing all day. The schools were closed, but Lewis ______ home from work.

FUNKTIONEN

- vorübergehende Handlung
- Beschreibung der Szene und Hintergrundhandlungen
- nach *while*

think

FUNKTION: ______

2. Lewis ______ for a moment about how he could have some fun when he got home. Then he had an idea.

sit
watch

FUNKTION: ______

3. When he arrived home at five o'clock, his two sons ______ around doing nothing and ______ TV.

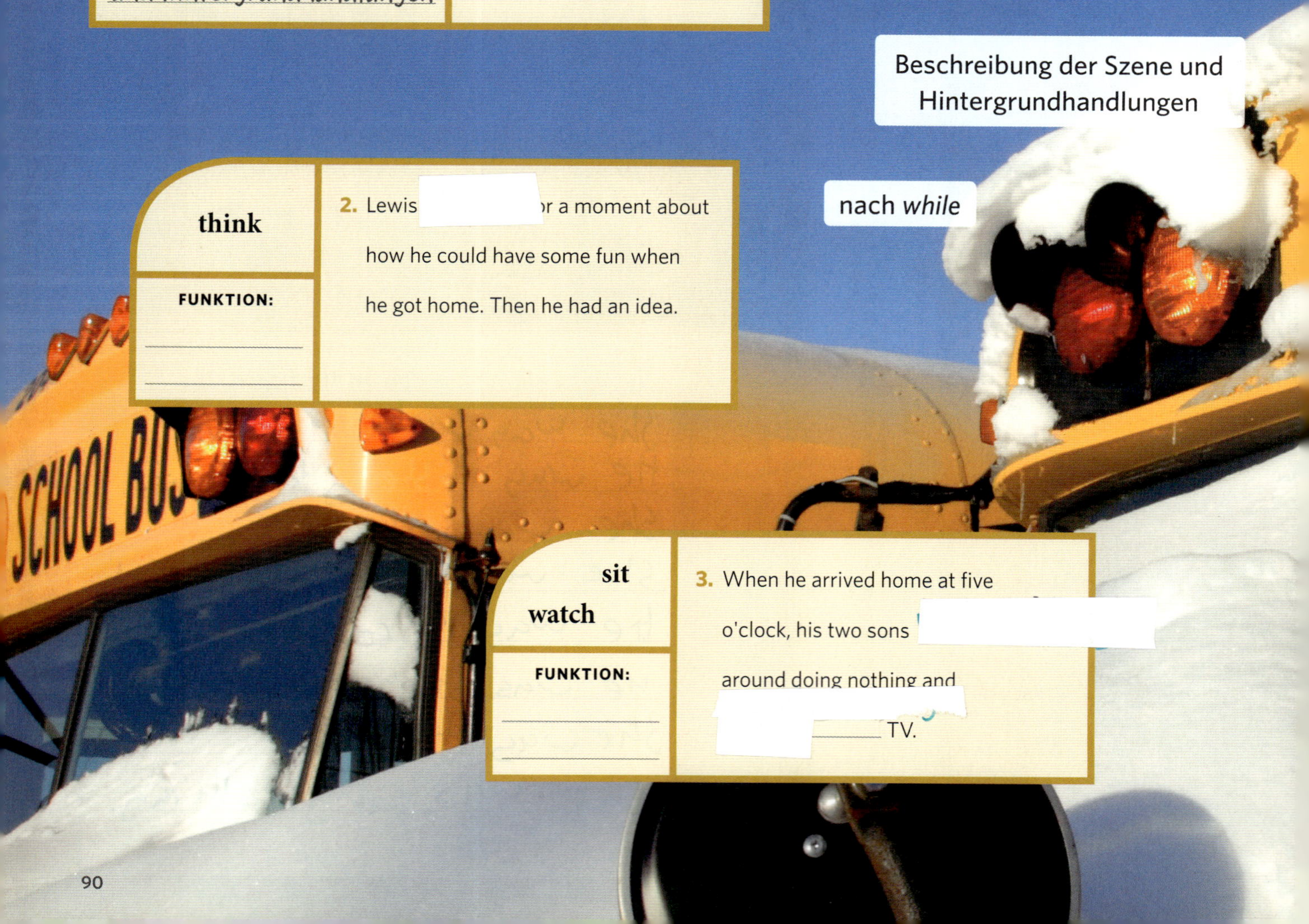

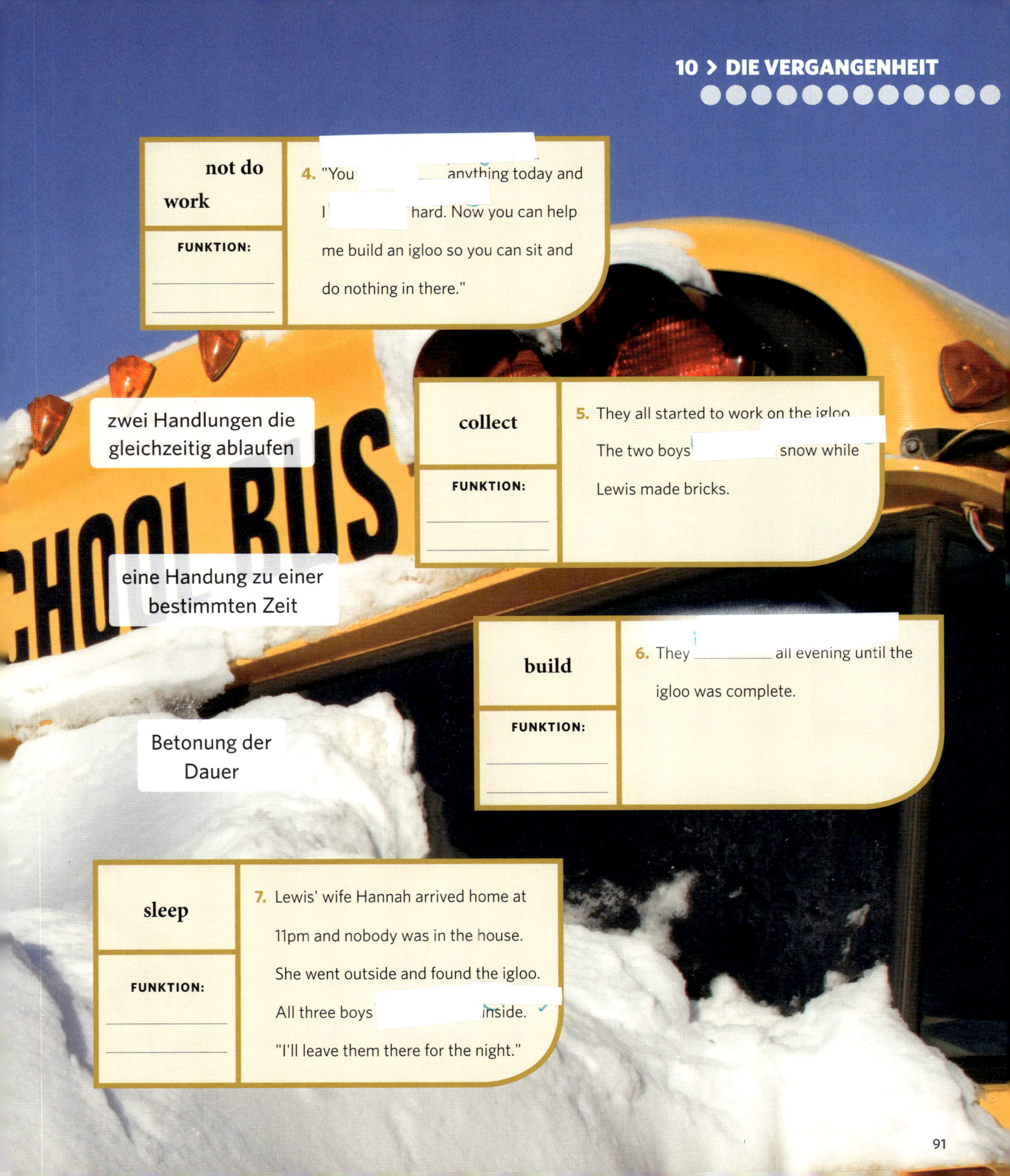

not do / work	4. "You __________ anything today and I __________ hard. Now you can help me build an igloo so you can sit and do nothing in there."
FUNKTION: __________	

zwei Handlungen die gleichzeitig ablaufen

collect	5. They all started to work on the igloo. The two boys __________ snow while Lewis made bricks.
FUNKTION: __________	

eine Handung zu einer bestimmten Zeit

build	6. They __________ all evening until the igloo was complete.
FUNKTION: __________	

Betonung der Dauer

sleep	7. Lewis' wife Hannah arrived home at 11pm and nobody was in the house. She went outside and found the igloo. All three boys __________ inside. "I'll leave them there for the night."
FUNKTION: __________	

8. Musik!

Schauen Sie sich die Songtexte an. Hier kommen sowohl das *past simple* als auch das *past progressive* vor. Leider sind die Vergangenheitsformen verloren gegangen.
Setzen Sie sie wieder ein. Sie können sich zur Unterstützung eine Zeichnung wie im Beispiel machen.
Überlegen Sie immer – wann finden die Handlungen statt?

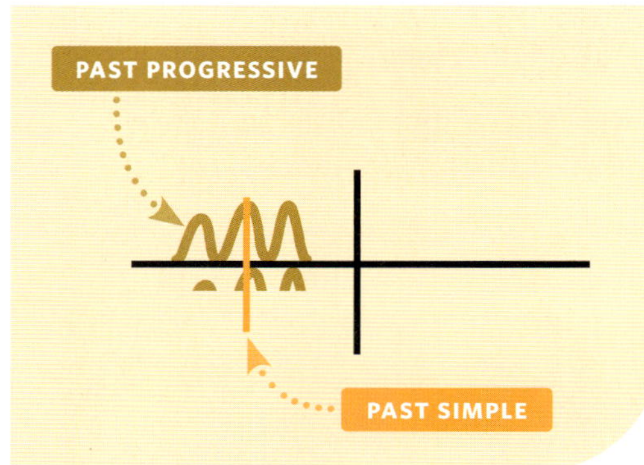

1 "You _were working_ (work) as a waitress in a cocktail bar, when I _met_ (meet) you."

THE HUMAN LEAGUE

2 "I ________ (hear) the mission bell, and I ________ (think) to myself this could be heaven or this could be hell."

THE EAGLES

3 "Slowly walking down the hall, faster than a cannonball. Where ________ (be) you while we ________ (get) high?"

OASIS

4 "I ________ (walk) down the street when out the corner of my eye I ________ (see) a pretty young thing approaching me."

CAGE THE ELEPHANT

5 "I ________ (cry) when I ________ (meet) you now I'm tryin' to forget you."

AEROSMITH

6 "I ________ (dream) of the past, and my heart ________ (beat) fast. I ________ (begin) to lose control."

JOHN LENNON

7 "What ______ you ______ (do) when I ________ (see) you last night? ______ you just ______ (play) hands? Or ______ he ________ (hold) you tight? "

JOHN LENNON

9. Es war einmal ... ein Fahrrad

Noch eine Möglichkeit der Wiedergabe der Vergangenheit ist das *past perfect*. Sie verwenden es für Handlungen und Ereignisse, die noch vor einem anderen Ereignis in der Vergangenheit stattfanden. Gebildet wird es mit der *past simple*-Form von *have* + *past participle*.
Lesen Sie den folgenden Dialog und füllen Sie die Lücken mit den richtigen *past perfect*-Formen.

10. Was geschah wann?

Helfen Sie, den Ablauf zu rekonstruieren. Schauen Sie sich die Ereignisse an und verorten Sie sie auf dem Zeitstrahl.

- He went to get an ice-cream.
- He forgot his bike key.
- Someone stole the bike.
- He arrived at the park.
- He cycled to the the park.
- He *realised* he had forgotten his bike key.
- He put the bike near the pond.

1. *He forgot his bike key.*
2. ______________________
3. ______________________
4. ______________________
5. ______________________
6. ______________________
7. ______________________

11. Immer dieses Warten

Und noch eine Möglichkeit über die Vergangenheit zu sprechen: das *past perfect progressive*. Sie verwenden es, wenn Sie von länger andauernden Handlungen sprechen, die vor einer anderen Handlung in der Vergangenheit stattgefunden haben. Gebildet wird es mit *be* im *past perfect* + *present participle*.

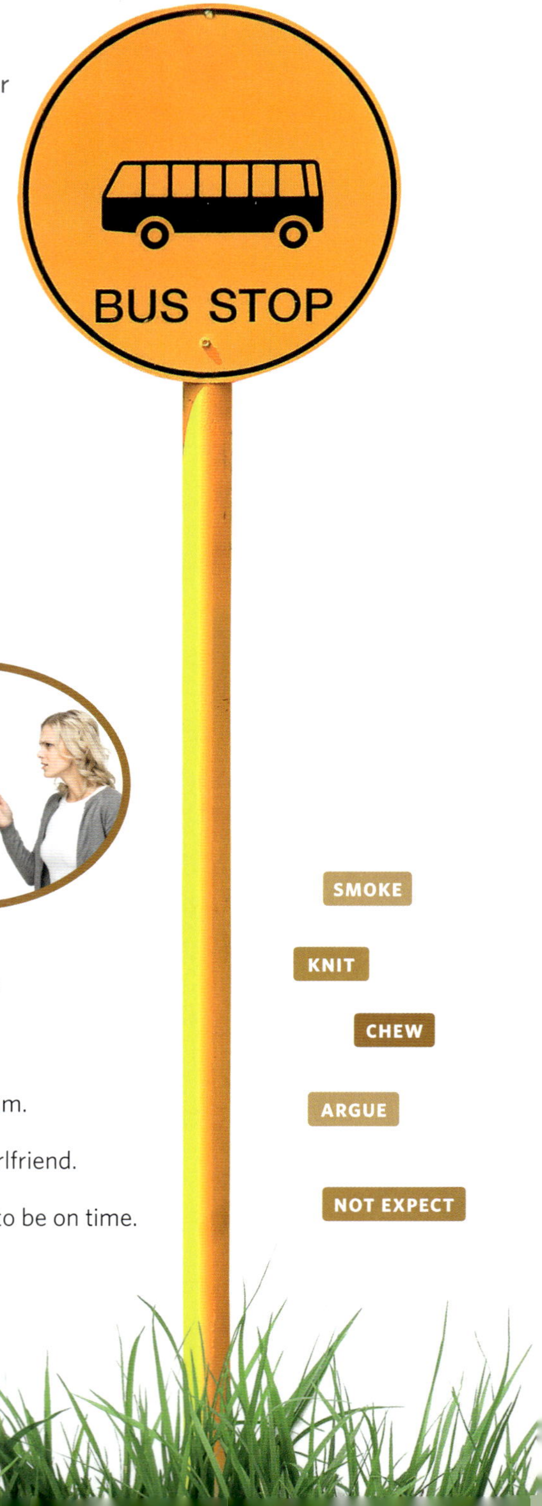

Was machten die Leute auf den Fotos, bevor der Bus kam? Füllen Sie die Lücken mit den angegebenen Verben im *past perfect progressive*.

1

2

3

4

5

1. He *had been smoking* a big cigar.
2. She ______________ a scarf.
3. She ______________ bubble gum.
4. He ______________ with his girlfriend.
5. They ______________ the bus to be on time.

SMOKE
KNIT
CHEW
ARGUE
NOT EXPECT

12. So viele Möglichkeiten

Vervollständigen Sie die Lücken mit dem *past simple*, dem *past perfect* oder dem *past perfect progressive*. Sie können sich selbst auch eine Grafik zeichnen.

1 They *had been waiting* (wait) for hours before the bus finally ____________ . (arrive)

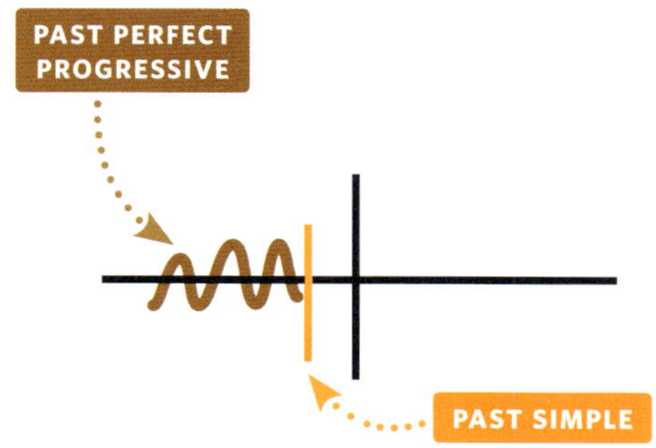

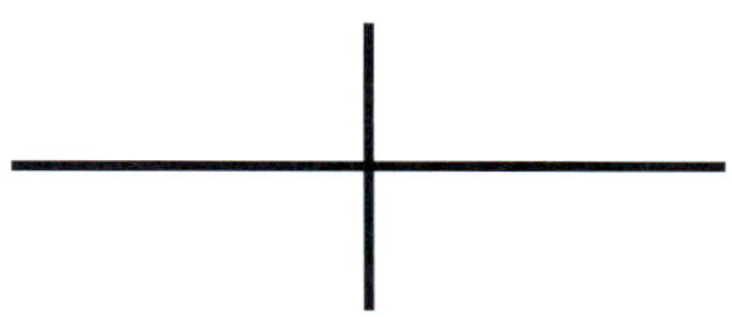

2 He ____________ (cut) the grass all afternoon when his lawnmower ____________ . (break)

3 Some students ____________ (finished) by the time the bell ____________ . (ring)

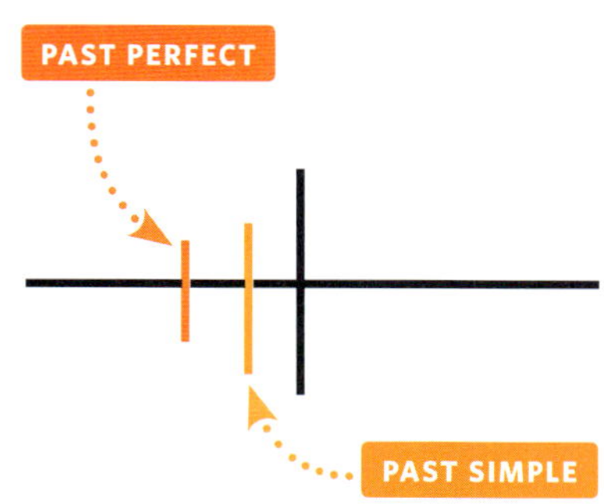

4 The family ____________ (eat) and ____________ (wash up) before the film ____________ . (begin)

13. Noch mehr Möglichkeiten

Und nun vervollständigen Sie die Lücken mit dem *past simple*, dem *past perfect* oder dem *past progressive*. Sie können sich selbst auch eine Grafik zeichnen.

1

He *had been looking* (look) for for his keys for an hour before he ______________ (find) them.

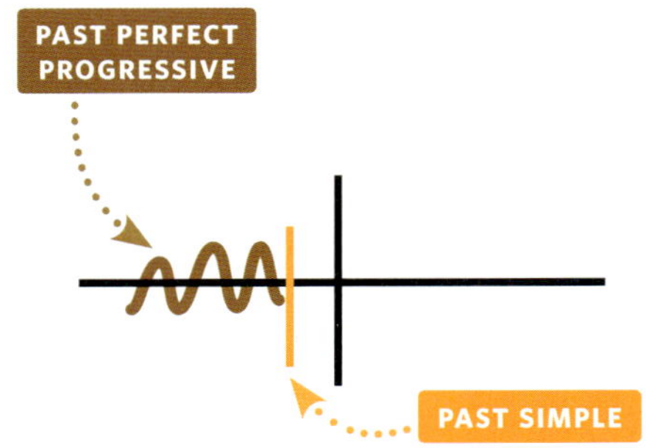

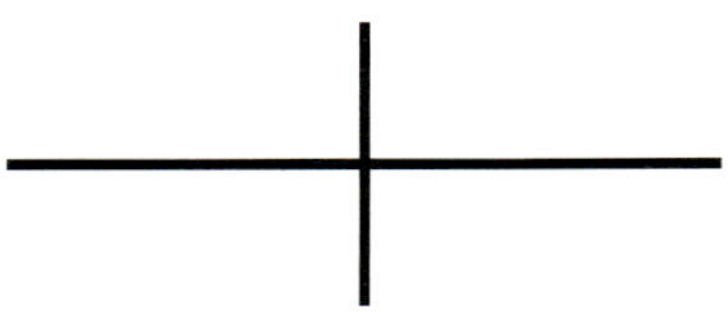

She ______________ (met) him after she ______________ (living) in London for five years.

2

3

He ______________ (look) for his keys when he ______________ (find) the money.

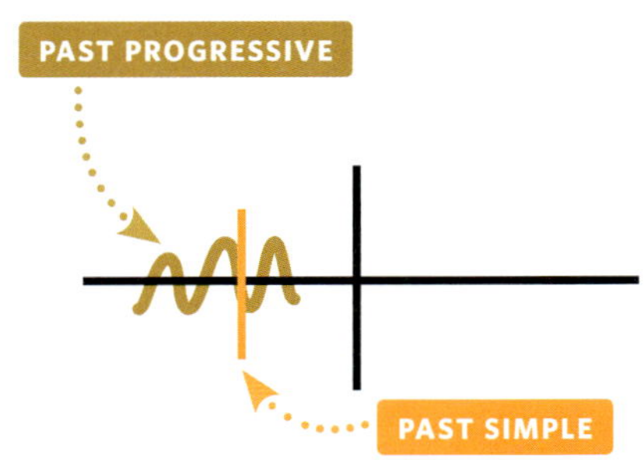

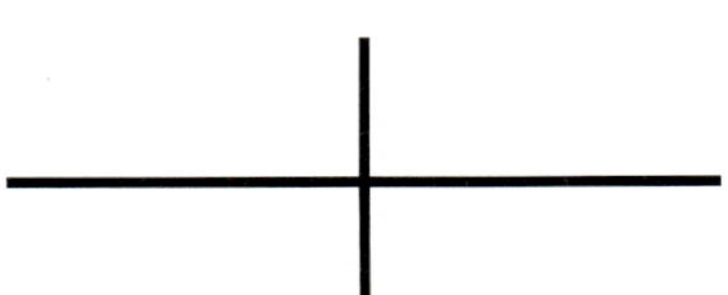

They ______________ (marry) each other while they ______________ (live) in London.

4

14. Etwas fehlt

Sie dachten, Sie hatten schon alle Vergangenheitsformen durch? Fast! Hier noch eine: das *present perfect*. Es wird für Ereignisse verwendet, die sich in der Vergangenheit abspielten, aber noch in der Gegenwart von Bedeutung sind. Gebildet wird es mit einer Form von *have* im *present simple* + *past participle*.

Hier sind einige Puzzlestücke verlorengegangen. Setzen Sie die passenden wieder ein, um Sätze im *present perfect* zu bilden.

Have — haven't. — has — Hasn't — hasn't.

1 Have you called your mother?

2 No, I

3 She ... tried to call you 3 times. today!

4 ... she got anything better to do?

5 No, she

15. *Past Participle*

Vervollständigen Sie alle Reihen mit dem *past particple*.

	INFINITIVE	PAST SIMPLE	PAST PARTICIPLE
1	be	was/were	been
2	catch	caught	
3	drive	drove	
4	forget	forgot	
5	go	went	
6	know	knew	
7	make	made	
8	see	saw	

16. Signalwörter

Vervollständigen Sie die Lücken mit den passenden Zeitadverbien und bilden Sie Sätze mit dem *present perfect*.

since | for | just | already | so far | never | ever | yet

1

We've been friends since we met in high school.

2

He's ______ 10 fish ______ this morning.

3

They've ______ ______ on this road before.

4

Have you ______ ______ your child's birthday?

5

She's ______ ______ to meet her friend for coffee.

6

They've ______ each other ______ 50 years.

7

He hasn't ______ the bed ______.

8

I've ______ this film ______.

17. *Present perfect* oder *past simple?*

Was gehört in die Lücken – *present perfect* oder *past simple?*

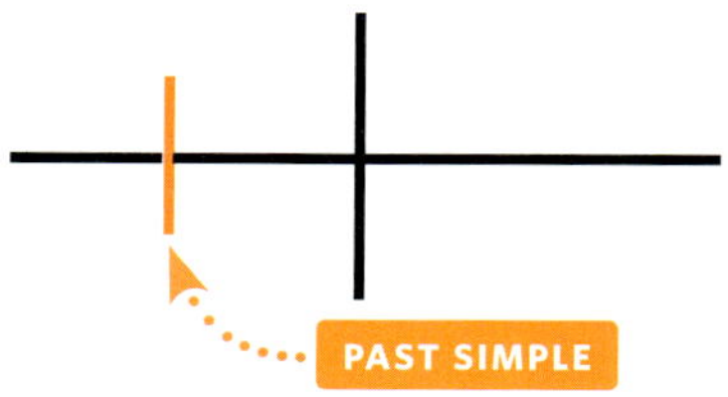

1 I __________ (work) as a waiter when I was fifteen. It was my first job.

2 I __________ (stay) in my first job for five years and I learnt all about the restaurant industry.

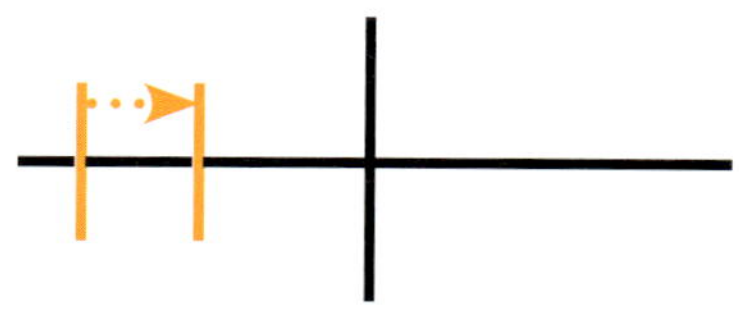

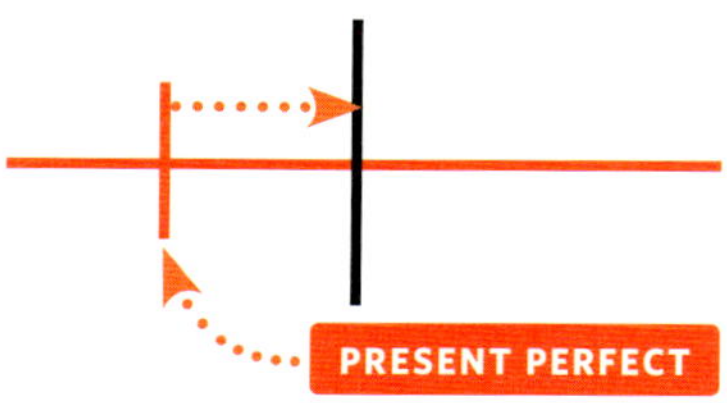

3 Now things are different. I __________ (work) as a restaurant critic for five years.

4 I __________ (eat) many fantastic meals in some of the best restaurants in the world.

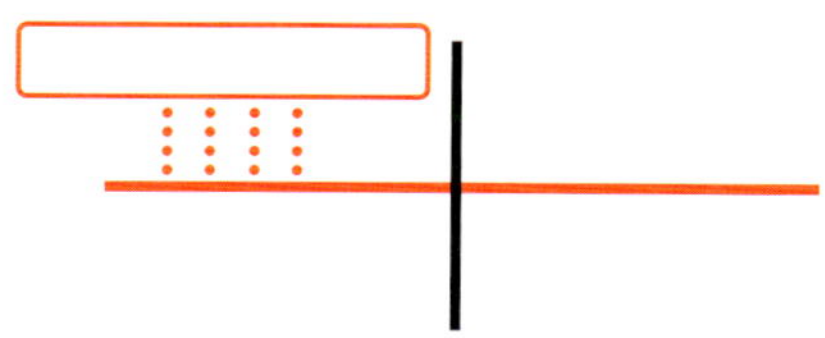

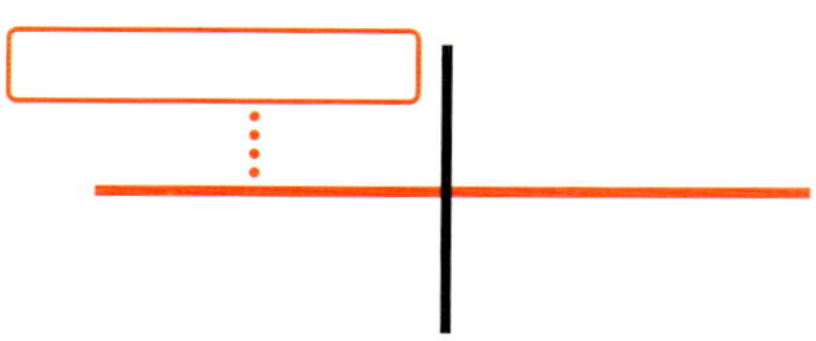

5 I __________ (try) food made by the world's top chef!

18. *Present perfect* oder *past simple?*

Hier stellt sich dieselbe Frage: *present perfect* oder *past simple?*

1

I ____________ (work) as a chef for the past 12 years.

2

When I was 16 I ____________ (get) my first job as a wash-up boy.

3

Then I ____________ (study) culinary arts in Toronto for 3 years.

4

Since then, I ____________ (have) many different jobs and I've been reviewed by many critics.

5

The world's top food writer ____________ (review) me. I hate restaurant critics!

19. Was taten sie?

Schauen Sie die Bilder an und bilden Sie Aussagesätze mit den angegebenen Verben im *present perfect progressive*.

What have they been doing?

1. She has been painting. — **paint**
2. ______ — **exercise**
3. ______ — **drink**
4. ______ — **not listen**

---

20. Ja oder nein?

Betrachten Sie auch hier die Fotos und bilden Sie Fragen und Kurzantworten. Verwenden Sie das *present perfect progressive*.

1. Has she been crying?
   Yes, she has. — **cry**
2. ______
   ______ — **do yoga**
3. ______
   ______ — **study**
4. ______
   ______ — **climb**

Have they ... ?

21. Was hat Max wie lange getan?

Max war und ist immer gut beschäftigt. Schauen Sie sich das Diagramm an und bilden Sie Sätze wie im Beispiel. Verwenden Sie das *present perfect progressive* und die Zeitangaben in den Kreisen.

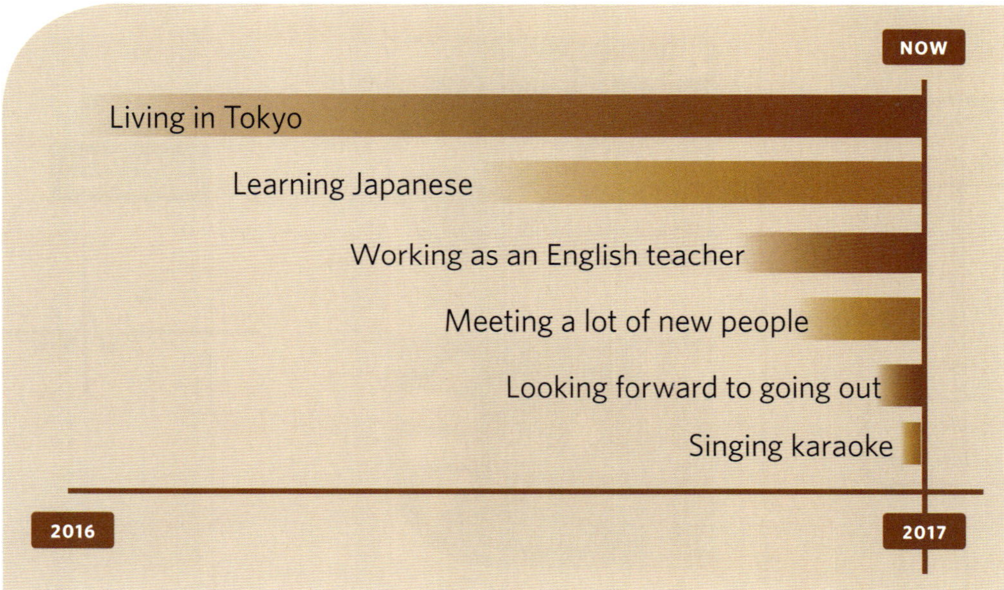

for 6 months | lately | all night | since 2016 | for 3 months | all week

1. *He's been living in Tokyo since 2016.*
2. ______
3. ______
4. ______
5. ______
6. ______

22. *Present progressive* oder *present perfect progressive?*

Ordnen Sie die Sätze zuerst dem passenden Bild zu und verbinden Sie sie dann mit der richtigen Grafik, um den Unterschied zwischen *present progressive* und *present perfect progressive* zu sehen.

1. I can't talk right now, I'm working.

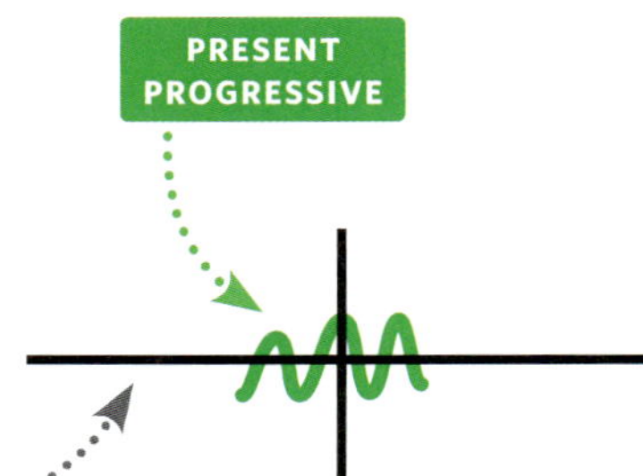

2. I've been feeling stressed all afternoon.

3. I'm speaking to a customer. Can I call you back?

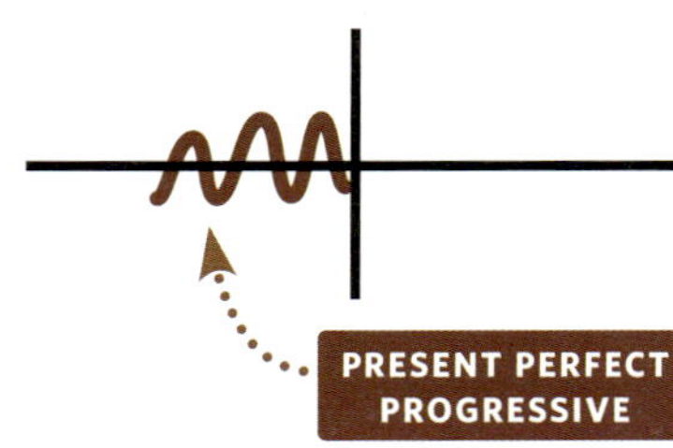

4. I'm so tired. I've been working hard all day.

23. So viele Möglichkeiten

Gehen Sie vor wie bei Übung 22. Diesmal geht es um den Unterschied zwischen *present perfect* und *present perfect progressive*.

1. She's written 3 best selling novels already.

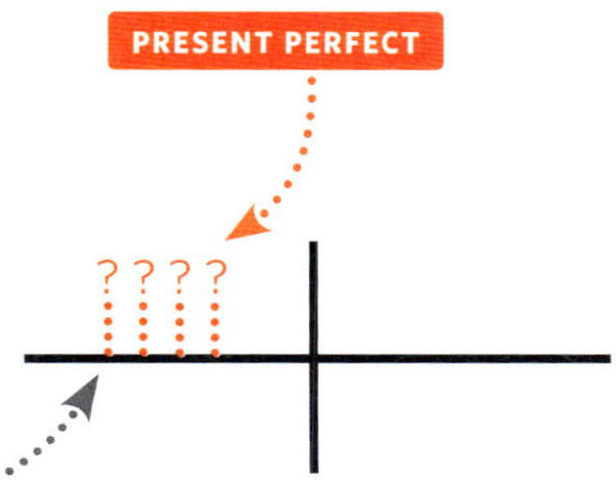

2. She's been working on her latest story.

3. She's written four chapters so far.

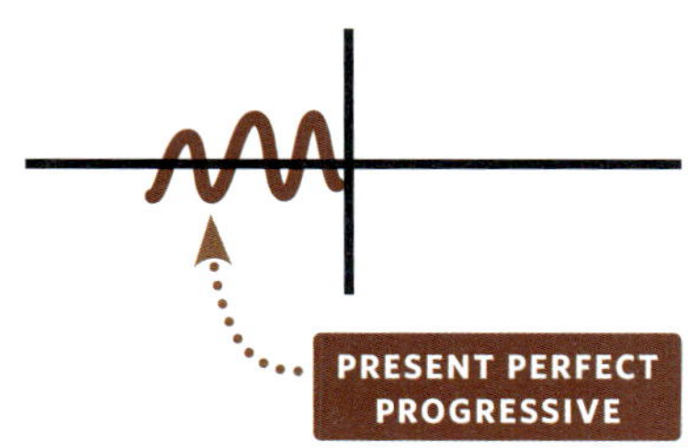

4. She's been typing all night.

11 Die Gegenwart

Wie kann ich im Englischen die Gegenwart ausdrücken?

Wozu kann ich die Zeiten der Gegenwart verwenden?

Wie **bilde** ich die Formen der Gegenwart?

now, when?

1. Das *present simple*

Die Gegenwart können Sie im Englischen mit dem *present simple* ausdrücken.
Schauen Sie sich die Bilder an und vervollständigen Sie die Sätze mit dem Verb in der korrekten Form.
Verwenden Sie auch Kurzformen.

live | love | not be | enjoy | can | dress | go | do | have

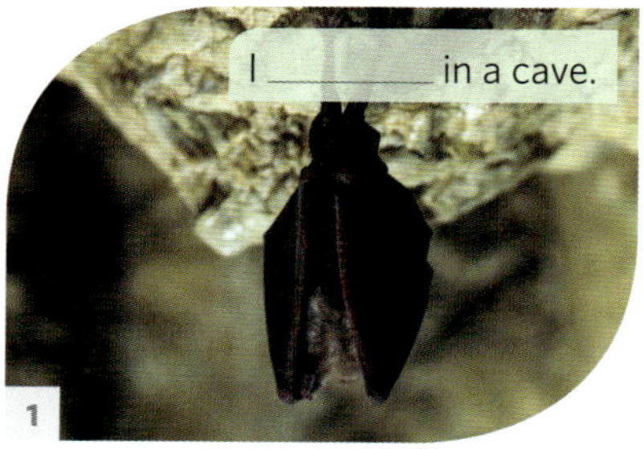

1

2

3

4

5

6

7

8

9

2. Ein bisschen anders

Wenn Sie das Modalverb *do* verwenden, müssen Sie auf die besonderen Formen in der 3. Person Singular, der Verneinung und Fragestellung achten. Vervollständigen Sie die Sätze unten. Verwenden Sie Kurzformen.

do	does	don't	doesn't
x 2	x 1	x 2	x 2

1. Does he know how to fly? I ______!

2. He can fly, but he ______ know how to drive!

3. And he ______ dress as well as me!

4. ______ you like my tights?

5. ______ you want to fight?

6. You ______ want to fight with me!

3. Klare Signale

Das *present simple* verwendet man nach bestimmten Signalwörtern. Hier sind einige davon. Können Sie sie in die richtigen Lücken einsetzen? Entscheiden Sie dann, welche der untenstehenden Funktionen zutrifft.

usually | if | every weekend | always | in a few days

1

Funktion:

She performs ________ ________.

2

Funktion:

Her next show is ________.

3

Funktion:

She ________ warms up before going on stage.

4

Funktion:

She ________ gets a burger and a milkshake after the show.

5

Funktion:

________ the show goes well, she gets a piece of pie as well!

Then she needs to enjoy herself...

regelmäßiges Ereignis | Konditional *(if+present simple)* | geplante Ereignisse in der Zukunft

4. Mittendrin!

Eine weitere Möglichkeit, die Gegenwart im Englischen wiederzugeben, ist das *present progressive*. Damit können Sie Ereignisse beschreiben, die gerade im Moment passieren. Erinnern Sie sich an die Bildung? Ganz einfach: die passende Form von *to be* + die Grundform des Verbs *(present participle)*. Bilden Sie die Formen unten nach dem Beispiel – immer mit *he*.

		+	-	?
1 	fly	He's flying.	He's not flying.	Is he flying?
2 	fight			
3 	balance			
4 	get angry			
5 	hang			

5. Noch mehr Signale

Auch für das *present progressive* gibt es Signalwörter, die es Ihnen einfacher machen, es richtig einzusetzen. Hier einige davon. Setzen Sie die richtigen Wörter in die Lücken und verbinden Sie die Kästchen anschließend mit dem passenden Zeitstrahl.

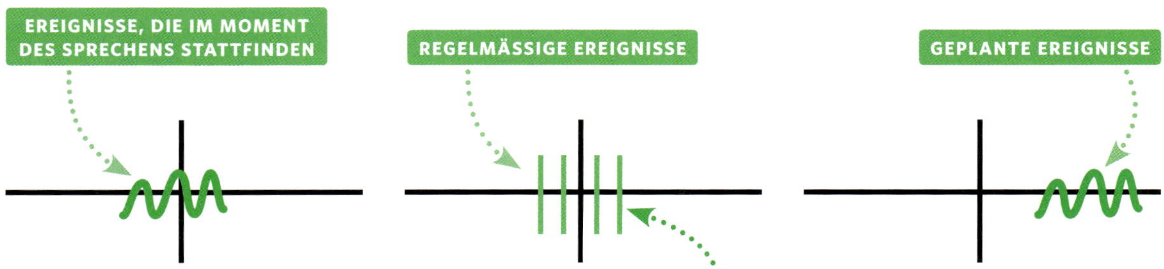

1 Those boys are always pretending.

6 Are we driving or flying to dinner ______ ______?

2 We're watching the new Batman film ______ ______.

always
at the moment
right now
tomorrow
this evening
always

5 Mr Hulk is ______ losing his temper.

3 I can't talk ______ ______ ______. I'm saving the world.

4 I'm meeting Ms Wonder for lunch ______!

6. *Present simple* oder *present progressive*?

Die Frage, ob etwas gerade eben passiert oder ob es sich um Ereignisse handelt, die regelmäßig stattfinden, hilft Ihnen dabei zu entscheiden, ob Sie *present simple* oder *present progressive* verwenden müssen. Achten Sie auch auf Signalwörter und verbinden Sie die passenden Sätze.

1. The local dog show happens → **B.**

2. Our bulldog starts feeling excited

3. At the moment

4. We're leaving for the show

5. Sometimes

6. But most of the time

7. The problem is: our bulldog

A. we win a prize.

B. once a year in September.

C. is always eating so much that he can't stand up!

D. every year around late August.

E. we don't.

F. early tomorrow morning.

G. we're trying on outfits for the show.

12 Die Zukunft

Welche Zukunftsformen gibt es im Englischen?

Wann verwende ich **welche** Form?

Wie wird die Zukunft im Englischen gebildet?

1. Wochenendpläne

Schauen Sie sich Marys Pläne für das Wochenende an und beantworten Sie die Fragen. Verwenden Sie das *going-to-future.*

1. What's Mary going to do on Saturday afternoon? *She's going to go to town and have coffee.*
2. What's Mary going to do on Saturday evening? ______________________
3. ______________________ run on Sunday aftenoon? (Vervollständigen Sie die Frage.)
4. What's Mary not going to do on Sunday morning? *She's not going to...*
5. What's Mary going to buy at the market? ______________________
6. What's Mary going to eat on Sunday evening? ______________________

2. Was hat sie vor?

Vervollständigen Sie nun die Sätze mit dem *going-to-future progressive*.
Dieses beschreibt etwas, das in der Zukunft geplant ist.

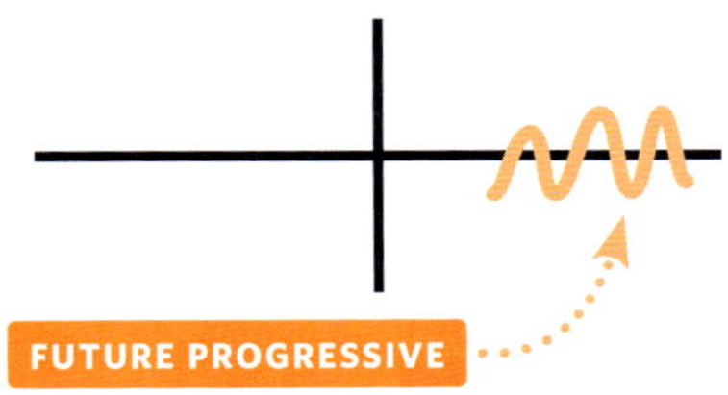

1. On Saturday morning...
   She's going to be buying fresh fish.

2. On Sunday evening...
   ____

3. On Sunday afternoon...
   ____

3. Fragen über Fragen

Üben Sie nun die Verneinung und die Fragestellung.

	-	?
1.	She's not going to be buying fresh fish.	Is she going to be buying fresh fish?
2.		
3.		

4. Für jedes Wetter gewappnet

Ordnen Sie Aussagen den passenden Bildern zu.

take a scarf and gloves | wear sunglasses | wrap up warm

take an umbrella | wear wellies | put on suncream

5. Wie wird das Wetter?

Beschreiben Sie das Wetter bei 2. und 3. indem Sie Sätze mit dem *going-to-future progressive* bilden. Erklären Sie dann bei 4. – 6. wie sie planen, sich aufgrund des Wetters auszustatten. Benutzen Sie dabei die Phrasen aus Übung 4.

ON MONDAY

ON TUESDAY

ON WEDNESDAY

1. It's going to be raining.
2. ____________________
3. ____________________

4. I'm going to take an umbrella.
5. ____________________
6. ____________________

6. Das *will-future*

Eine andere Möglichkeit im Englischen über die Zukunft zu sprechen ist das *will-future*.
Es wird verwendet, wenn etwas in der Zukunft als sicher gilt. Sie bilden es mit *will/won't* + Infinitv.
Setzen Sie in den Beispielen unten die korrekten Formen ein.

will	'll	won't
x 5	x 2	x 2

1.

_______ you dance with me?

Yes, _______.

She _______ dance with him.

2.

_______ you go to dinner with me?

Yes, _______.

She _______ go to dinner with him.

3.

_______ you marry me?

No, I _______.

She _______ marry him.

7. Das *will-future progressive*

Das *will-future progressive* beschreibt etwas, was zu einem angegebenen Zeitpunkt mit großer Sicherheit im Gange, aber noch nicht abgeschlossen sein wird. Es wird gebildet mit *will* + *be* + *ing*-Form. Lesen Sie die Sprechblasen und beschreiben Sie das Bild, wie in Beispiel 1, indem Sie das *will-future progressive* verwenden.

1. On Friday night/dance/at the concert

1

On Friday night she'll be dancing at the concert

2. In two hours/walk/in the forest

2

3. This time tomorrow/swim/ in the sea

3

4. On Sunday afternoon/play football/with my son

4

8. Berühmte Zitate

Hier sehen Sie eine Reihe von bekannten Zitaten. Vervollständigen Sie sie mit den angegebenen Satzteilen. Ordnen Sie anschließend jedem Zitat eine der auf S. 125 (unten) angegebenen Funktionen des *will-futures* zu.

...will never be content.

...will be famous for 15 minutes.

...will be successful.

...will never walk alone.

...will be sunshine.

...will never reach your destination.

...will never get out of it alive.

1
"You
will never walk alone
Oscar Hammerstein II
verprechen

2
"If you love what you're doing, you...
____
Albert Schweiter
____

3
"Don't take life too seriously, you...
____
____
Elbert Hubbard
____

4
"In the future, everyone...
____
Andy Warhol
____

5

"If you look for perfection, you

____

Leo Tolstoy

6

"Never give up. Today is hard, tomorrow will be worse, but the day after tomorrow ...

____

Jack Ma

7

"You

____

if you stop and throw stones at every dog that barks."

Winston Churchill

VERWENDUNG IM KONDITIONALSATZ MIT *IF*

VORHERSAGEN/TATSACHEN IN DER ZUKUNFT

VERSPRECHEN

9. Safari!

Hier ist einiges geplant! Schauen Sie sich links die Reiseplanung der Safaritouristen an und bilden Sie anschließend rechts Sätze, indem Sie das *present simple* oder *present progressive* verwenden. Ersteres verwenden Sie, wenn es um Ereignisse in der Zukunft ohne fest geplanten Zeitpunkt geht. Letzteres für geplante Ereignisse.

Weekend Safari Schedule

Day 1

9.00 – Train: Manchester to London

13.00 – Plane: London to Johannesburg

18.00 – Arrive in Johannesburg

19.00 – Taxi to the hotel

21.00 – Dinner with safari group

Day 2

7.00 – Wake up

9.00 – Bus to Kruger National Park

11.30 – The safari

18.00 – A meeting with a rhino expert

21.00 – A photo sharing session

1. leave Our train leaves at 9.00.
2. take off ______
3. arrive ______
4. take ______
5. have ______
6. wake up ______
7. leave ______
8. start ______
9. have ______
10. go to ______

10. Was die wohl getan haben werden?

Mit dem *future perfect* können Sie über Ereignisse sprechen, die zu einem bestimmten Zeitpunkt schon stattgefunden haben werden. Sie bilden es mit dem Hilfsverb *will* + *have* + *past participle* des Verbs. Versuchen Sie es hier gleich einmal!

By 8 am …

his cows | milked | will | have | He

1. He will have milked his cows.

will | He | have | breakfast | had

2. ______________________________

bed | gone | They | won't | have | to

3. ______________________________

gone | he | have | Will | for a run | ?

4. ______________________________

11. Und was die wohl immer noch tun werden?

Mit dem *future perfect progressive* sprechen Sie über Ereignisse, die zu einem gegebenen Zeitpunkt immer noch im Gange sein werden bzw. über Zustände, die immer noch andauern werden. Bilden Sie Sätze wie in Übung 10.

By 11 am ...

will | been | cutting the grass | have | He | for 2 hours

1. He will have been cutting the grass for 2 hours.

have | working | been | will | He | for 2 hours

2. ______

They | sleeping | have | for an hour | will | been

3. ______

he | been | running | Will | ? | have | for 5 minutes

4. ______

12. Schon fertig?

Verbinden Sie die Sätze mit den passenden Bildern, um zu entscheiden, ob es sich um abgeschlossene Ereignisse handelt oder solche, die noch im Gange sind. Achtung: die Bilder passen zu mehreren Sätzen.

noch im Gange

abgeschlossen

noch im Gange

abgeschlossen

1. By 12, she will have been flying for 5 hours.
2. They'll be watching the game at the moment.
3. She'll be flying to London now.
4. They will have finished watching the game.
5. She'll be in London by now.
6. They will have been watching the game since 3pm.
7. She will have arrived in London by now.
8. They game will be over by now.

13. Will-future oder going-to-future?

Schauen Sie sich die unterschiedlichen Funktionen von *will* und *going to* an. Verbinden Sie anschließend die Sätze mit den passenden Funktionen.

VERSPRECHEN → ______

ENTSCHEIDUNG → ______

PLAN/ABSICHT → ______

VORHERSAGE → *We'll probably eat...* / ______

1. "We'll probably eat around 7pm."

2. "I think it's going to taste pretty good."

3. "Dinner's ready. I'll set the table."

4. "We're going to have trifle for dessert."

5. "I'll cook next time, I swear."

14. Will-future oder going-to-future?

Hier sehen Sie berühmte Filmzitate. Entscheiden Sie, welche der in Übung 14 genannten Funktionen hier zutreffen.

"All these moments will be lost in time, like tears in the rain."
BLADE RUNNER
1. Versprechen

"I'll be back."
THE TERMINATOR
2. ____________

"I'm gonna make him an offer he can't refuse."
THE GODFATHER
3. ____________

"You're gonna need a bigger boat."
JAWS
4. ____________

"I'll have what she's having."
WHEN HARRY MET SALLY
5. ____________

"I will have my vengeance in this life or the next."
GLADIATOR
6. ____________

15. Du sollst nicht ...

Auch mit *shall* kann man teilweise die Zukunft ausgedrücken. Es kann daneben auch verwendet werden, wenn man Befehle gibt, die nicht nur die Zukunft, sondern auch die Gegenwart betreffen. Darüber hinaus kann man mit *shall* auch fragen, ob man etwas unternehmen will. Bilden Sie Sätze wie im Beispiel.

You must not kill. → 1. *You shall not kill.*

How about going out for dinner? → 2. ______________________

Do you want me to clean it? → 3. ______________________

You must obey me! → 4. ______________________

Do you want to do something? → 5. ______________________

16. Wenn - dann

Zukunftsformen begegnen einem auch oft in Bedingungssätzen mit *if* oder *when*.
Vervollständigen Sie die Bedingungssätze mit den unten angegebenen Formen des *will-future*.

1. If you cook the main course, *I'll make dessert.*
2. If I make dinner, ______________________
3. If we're working late tonight, ______________________
4. If you've already eaten, ______________________
5. When you've learnt to cook, ______________________

we'll order a takeaway.

I'll make dessert.

you'll have to make me dinner.

will you do the washing up?

I'll just make myself a salad.

17. Vorfreude und gute Vorsätze

Dieses Pärchen freut sich auf aufregende Tage in Las Vegas. Was haben sie dort vor? Benutzen Sie das *going-to-* oder *will-future* um die Sätze zu vervollständigen.

"We're excited because

we are going to (go to)

Las Vegas!"

"We think

_______________ (be)

the time of our lives."

"We have a feeling

_______________ (win)

big!"

"We promise

_______________ (not do)

anything stupid."

18. Und dann kam alles anders

Manchmal laufen die Dinge anders als geplant. Was berichtet unser Pärchen? Verwenden Sie *was/were going-to-* oder *would* um Aussagen über die Zukunft in der Vergangenheit zu machen.

"We were excited because we were going to (go to) Las Vegas."

1

2

"We thought ______ (be) the time of our lives."

"We had a feeling ______ (win) big!

3

4

"We promised ______ (not do) anything stupid."

13 Der Konditional

Was ist der Konditional?

Was **drücke ich** damit **aus**?

Wie bilde den Konditional?

I wish
I could fly...

1. Was wäre wenn?

Wenn Sie im Englischen eine Bedingung wiedergeben wollen, verwenden Sie das *conditional*. Sie bilden es mit *would* + Infinitiv. Bilden Sie Sätze wie im Beispiel.

If it snowed tomorrow,

...I would go skiing.

I'd go skiing

...I would not be happy.

______

...she would make some soup.

______

...he would not get to work.

______

...he would build an igloo.

______

...we would not have to go to school.

______

2. Wollen wir nicht?

Formulieren Sie nun Fragen - positive und verneinte. Achten Sie auf die Stellung des Subjekts!

Go sledging?

1. Would we go sledging?
2. ______

Build a snowman?

3. ______
4. ______

3. Wenn nicht so viele wenns wären

Susan ist in Partystimmung - oder doch nicht? Schreiben Sie, unter welchen Bedingungen sie auf die Party gehen würde und was sie davon abhält. Verwenden Sie das *conditional* mit Infinitiv. Vergessen Sie nicht: *no would in the if-clause!*

if + past simple		but + present simple
1. you/drive	2. you/come/with me	5. I/not/have time
3. I/have/a car	4. I/not/have to work	6. I/not/feel like partying

I would go to the party...

4. Ein Wort, viele Funktionen

Mit *would* + Infinitiv kann man, außer Bedingungen, einige andere Dinge ausdrücken. Schauen Sie sich die Beschreibungen an und ordnen Sie sie den passenden Bildern zu.

A Ratschläge erteilen.

B hypothetische Fragen stellen

C über die Vergangenheit sprechen

D höfliche Bitten formulieren

If I were you, I would see a doctor.

1

We would play in the garden all the time when we were young.

2

Would you please close the window?

3

Would you ever eat snails?

4

5. Das *conditional progressive*

Wenn Sie über Dinge sprechen möchten, die aufgrund eingetretener Ereignisse oder Zustände nicht passiert sind, verwenden Sie das *conditional progressive*. Sie bilden es mit *would + be + ing*-Form. Bilden Sie Sätze wie im Beispiel.

If the volcano was active,

1. *we'd be living in a dangerous place.* — we/live/in a dangerous place
2. .... — we/think/about moving house

3. .... — he/not/climb it
4. .... — he/not/feel so relaxed

5. .... — they/take a tour?
6. .... — they/look into the crater?

6. Vieles ist möglich

Mit *will, can, may* sowie *would, could* und *might* können Sie über Möglichkeiten in der Zukunft sprechen, die mehr oder weniger wahrscheinlich sind. Dabei liegt der Fokus immer anders. Lesen Sie die Informationen. Entscheiden Sie bei 1. – 3. was ausgedrückt wird. Lösen Sie dann 4. – 6.

Möglichkeit in der Zukunft

If I have time,

1. I **will** come with you.

2. I **can** come with you.

3. I **may** come with you.

A It's definite but conditional.

B It's possible.

C It's something I have the ability to do.

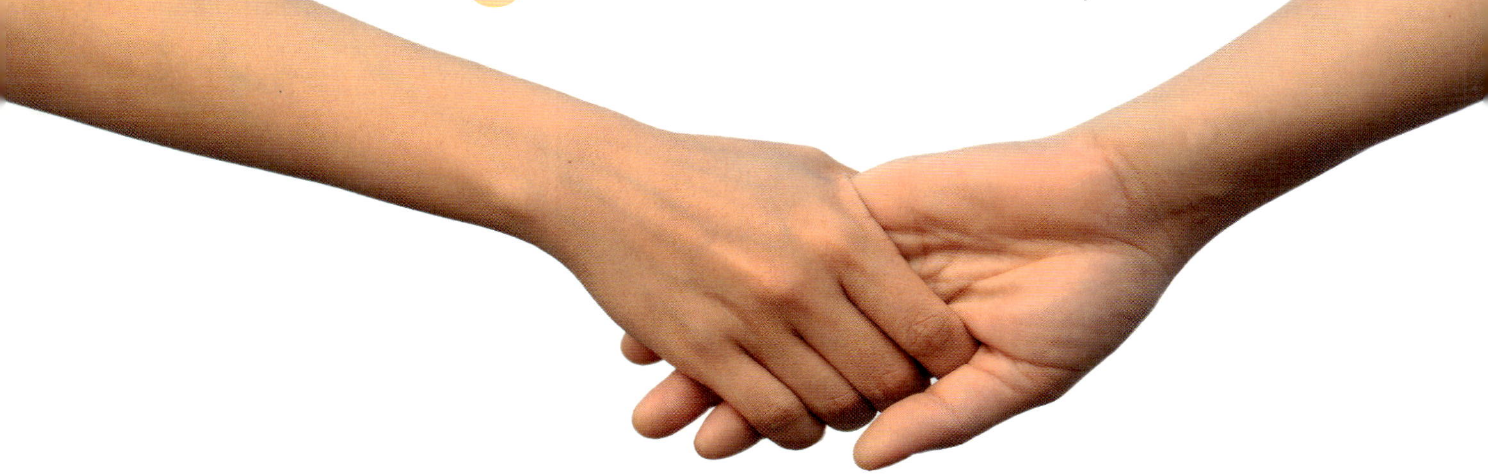

Hypothetische Möglichkeit in der Zukunft

If I had time,

4. will becomes ______________ I **would** come with you.

5. can becomes ______________ I **could** come with you.

6. may becomes ______________ I **might** come with you.

7. Träume über Träume

Schreiben Sie die Sätze um, indem Sie *would* durch *could* oder *might* ersetzen.

1. **...it's possible I would** buy that car.
   I might buy that car.

2. **...I would be able** to buy that car.

   ____

   ____

3. **...I would be able** to cruise with the top down.

   ____

   ____

4. ...**maybe I would** be driving it now.

   ____

   ____

8. Das *conditional perfect*

Das war ein Bier zu viel! Robin hat sein Vorstellungsgespäch verpasst und überlegt, was wohl gewesen wäre wenn ... Dafür bietet sich das *conditional perfect* an! Es wird verwendet, wenn man z.B. über Unmögliches in der Vergangenheit sprechen möchte. Man bildet es mit *would* + der Perfekt-Form des Verbs.

Führen Sie Robins Gedanken zu Ende und formulieren Sie positive und verneinende Sätze sowie Fragesätze. Pro Wortgruppe ergeben sich zwei Sätze.

If I hadn't drunk so much last night,

–

oversleep | would | I (x2) | might | miss my chance

?

get the job? | would | I | it | could | be a success?

+

wake up on time | would | I (x2) | would | make the interview

+

	SUBJECT	WOULD/COULD/MIGHT	HAVE	PAST PARTICIPLE
1.	I	would	have	woken up on time.
2.				

–

	SUBJECT	WOULD/COULD/MIGHT NOT	HAVE	PAST PARTICIPLE
3.				
4.				

?

	WOULD/COULD/MIGHT	SUBJECT	HAVE	PAST PARTICIPLE
5.				
6.				

9. Träume über Träume

Robin bereut seinen nächtlichen Ausflug noch immer. Vervollständigen Sie den Bedingungssatz mit den angegebenen Teilen aus den Kästchen.

if + past perfect		but + past simple
1. I/not meet Dom	2. I/not/go to the club	5. I/get too excited
3. I/remember the interview	4. my team/win the match	6. Dom/make me do shots

I wouldn't have drunk so much...

1. *if I hadn't met Dom.*

2.

3.

4.

5.

6.

10. Das *conditional perfect progressive*

Eine weitere Möglichkeit über Bedingungen zu sprechen, ist das *conditional perfect progressive*. Sie verwenden es, wenn Sie über Nicht-Eingetretenes in der Vergangenheit sprechen möchten. Gebildet wird es mit *would* + *have been* + *ing*-Form.

Mary hat ihren Flug verpasst – was für ein Jammer! Schreiben Sie, was sie getan hätte, wenn sie den Flieger erreicht hätte.

If she hadn't missed her flight,

she | lounging on the beach | been | would | have

1 *she would have been lounging on the beach.*

getting nice and brown | would | have | been | she

2 ______________________________

feeling miserable
she have not would
been

3 ______________________________

not would she been have
booking another holiday

4 ______________________________

have
enjoying herself?
she
wouldn't been

5 ______________________________

dancing with a stranger?
would been have she

6 ______________________________

11. *Conditional* und *conditional perfect*

Verbinden Sie die passenden Satzteile, um Sätze im *conditional* oder im *conditional perfect* zu erhalten. Tragen Sie anschließend unten ein, ob es sich um Aussagen in der hypothetischen Zukunft oder hypothetischen Vergangenheit handelt.

1. If I could go anywhere,

2. If I could have gone anywhere,

3. If I could take anybody with me,

4. If I could have taken anybody with me,

5. Would you come with me

6. Would you have come with me

A if I had asked you to come?

B I would go to Peru.

C I would take you.

D I would have taken you.

E I would have gone to Peru.

F if I asked you to come?

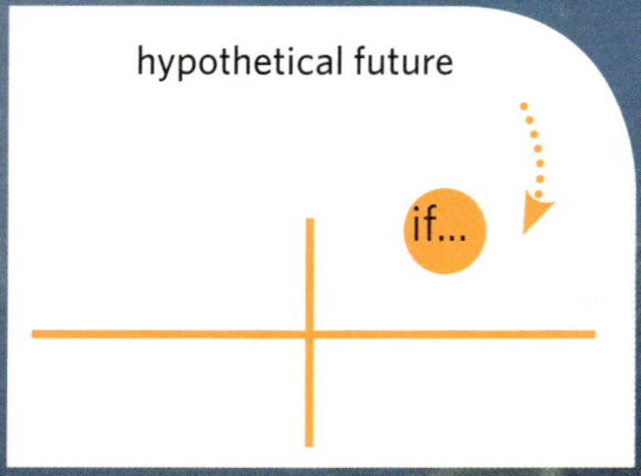

1B | ___ | ___

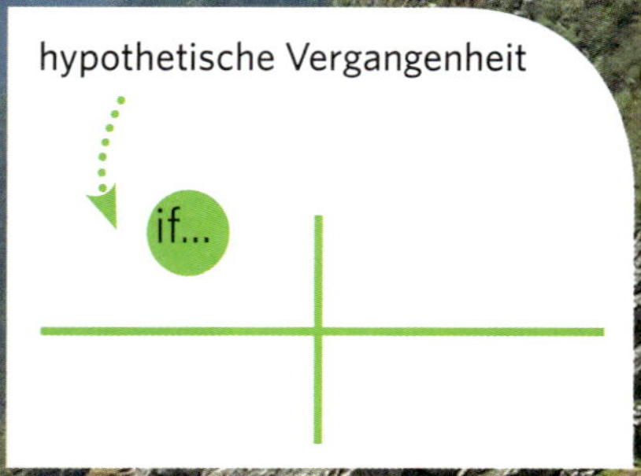

___ | ___ | ___

12. In der Kürze liegt die Würze

Schreiben Sie die Sätze von Übung 12, indem Sie Kurzformen verwenden.
In einem Fall ist keine Kurzform möglich.

1. *If I could go anywhere, I'd go to Peru.*
2.
3.
4.
5.
6.

14 Der Satzbau

Wie bilde ich einen englischen Satz?

Welche **Reihenfolge** haben die Satzglieder?

Was muss ich dabei beachten?

1. Feurige Teile

Damit Sie sich am englischen Satzbau nicht die Finger verbrennen, üben Sie hier die richtige Stellung. Nicht vergessen, im Aussagesatz lautet die Reihenfolge in der Regel: Subjekt – Verb – Objekt – (Ergänzung/Nebensatz).

Bringen Sie die Sätze in die richtige Reihenfolge und tragen Sie sie anschließend in die passenden Spalten der Tabelle auf der nächsten Seite ein.

1

2

3

4

They
food
for themselves.
could cook

5

They
dangerous animals.
were able to scare away

6

have found
Archaeologists
evidence of fire
from 700,000 years ago.

7

	SUBJEKT	VERB(EN)	OBJEKT	ERGÄNZUNG/NEBENSATZ
1	Humans	discovered	fire.	–
2		produces		
3	We			
4			an important step	
5				for themselves
6			dangerous animals	
7	Archaeologists			

2. Männer am Grill

Tony versucht sich an den Würstchen – mit mäßigem Erfolg. Sie sind sicher erfolgreicher, wenn es darum geht, die folgenden Sätze zu bilden. Schauen Sie sich die Bilder an. Wählen Sie dann aus jeder Box die Elemente, die Sie benötigen und bringen Sie alles in die richtige Reihenfolge, wie im Beispiel.

Ergänzung/Nebensatz

- Last weekend,
- because he fancies himself as a chef.
- Even though some of the sausages were burnt,

Subjekt

- My auntie
- it
- Uncle Tony
- my family

Verb

- did
- was
- had
- made

Objekt

- the cooking
- a barbeque.
- a nice afternoon
- everyone
- cocktails

1

Last weekend, my family had a barbeque.

2

3

4

3. Wer war's und wer will was?

Lesen Sie nun die Fragen und ordnen Sie anschließend deren Satzteile in die richtigen Kästen ein.

1 | How many sausages | did | you | eat? |

2 | Who | burnt | the sausages? |

3 | How much vodka | did | auntie | put | in the cocktails? |

4 | Is | anyone | still hungry? |

Ergänzung/ Nebensatz

- ______
- ______

Subjekt

- you
- ______
- ______
- ______

Verb

- did
- eat
- ______
- ______
- ______
- ______

Objekt

- How many sausages
- ______
- ______

4. Punkt und aus

Frischen Sie Ihre Kenntnisse zu den Satzzeichen im Englischen auf. Befolgen Sie die Anweisungen 1. – 6. in den folgenden kurzen Texten. Die Übung geht auf der nächsten Seite weiter!

1. In diesem Text fehlen Punkte, setzen Sie sie ein. Achten Sie auf Groß- und Kleinschreibung.

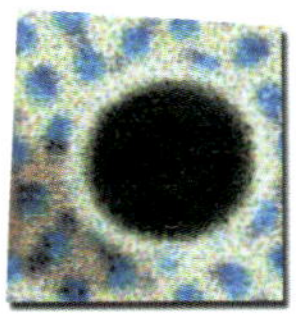

A full stop is used at the end of a sentence to be a sentence it must have a complete clause

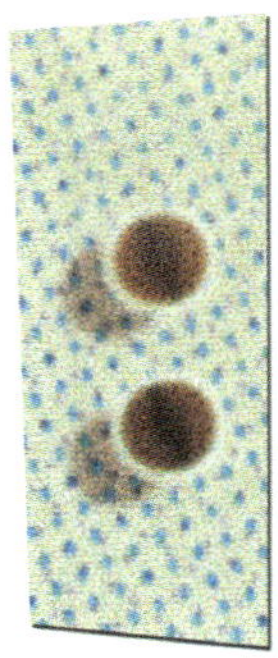

2. Wo gehört in diesem Text der Doppelpunkt hin?

There are two main rules about using colons don't use a capital letter after a colon and don't use a colon after an incomplete sentences.

3. Welcher Satz benötigt ein ! am Ende?

A Exclamation marks are used to express strong emotion

B Don't use exclamation marks the wrong way, you idiot

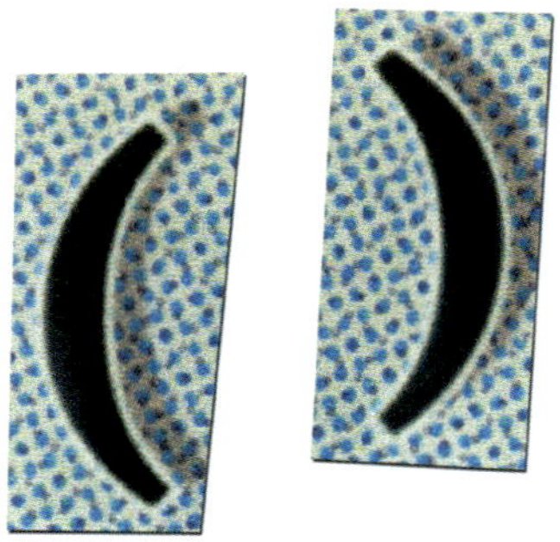

4. Dieser Text könnte Klammern vertragen. Wissen Sie wo?

Parenthesis sometimes called brackets are used to separate information which is not essential to the meaning of the sentence.

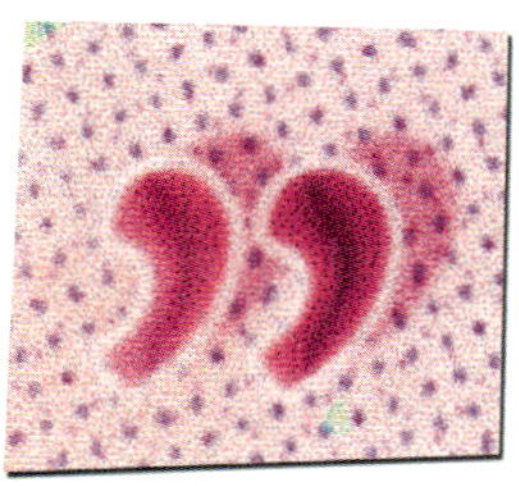

5. Fügen Sie Anführungszeichen ein.

We use quotation marks to present direct speech or an exact quote, my teacher said.

6. Welcher dieser Sätze benötigt ein ? am Ende?

A Question marks are marks which are used to ask a question

B Which sentence needs a question mark

5. Endlich zu Hause

Sam ist endlich daheim! Wer es noch nicht nach Hause geschafft hat, sind die Kommas, die im unteren Text fehlen. Setzen Sie sie ein – dann haben Sie erfolgreich ein weiteres Kapitel beendet!

After a long tiring day at work I eventually drove home. If I had been any more tired I would have fallen asleep at the wheel! In fact I was so exhausted that I drove on the wrong side of the road missed my turn off and I even went the wrong way round the roundabout. Nevertheless I managed to get home safely in the end.

15 Die Satzarten

Welche Arten von Sätzen gibt es im Englischen?

Wann verwende ich welche Satzart?

Was **drücke ich** mit

Should I call her?

1. Fragen und Antworten

Betrachten Sie die Fotos und bilden Sie aus den gegebenen Wörtern Ja-/Nein-Fragen und Antworten wie im Beispiel. Achten Sie auf die Wortstellung und die richtige Form des Verbs.

Present Simple

Fragen und Antworten mit *be*

1. the dog/tired?

Is the dog tired?

2. the dog/yes/tired

Yes, the dog is tired.

Fragen und Antworten mit *do*

3. 3. the dog/want a bone?

____

4. the dog/want a bone/no

____

Past Simple

Fragen und Antworten mit *can*

5. you/feed the dog?

____

6. you/help me find the turtle?

____

Fragen und Antworten mit *be*

7. the tank/open?

____

8. the turtles/inside?

____

Fragen und Antworten mit *do*

9. the turtle/escape?

____

10. you/forget to close the tank?

____

2. Wer, wo, was?

Fido ist ausgebüchst! Im Wortgitter sind sechs weitere Fragewörter versteckt. Finden Sie sie? Bilden Sie anschließend W-Fragen, indem Sie die passenden Fragewörter unten eintragen. Auch *how* wird einmal benötigt.

W	H	O	H	W	W
H	W	D	O	I	H
A	W	W	W	F	E
T	F	L	C	W	R
W	W	H	E	N	E
T	W	W	H	Y	P
W	H	I	C	H	M

1. Who … is your owner? / … do you answer to?

2. ______ … is your name? / … do you like to eat?

3. ______ … house is yours? / … way do you go?

4. ______ … are you all alone? / … don't you eat something?

5. ______ … were you going? / … did you come from?

6. ______ … was the last time you ate? / … did you last have a wash?

7. ______ … long were you lost for? / … did you end up here?

3. Alle Fragen geklärt?

Schauen Sie sich die Antworten in den Kreisen an. Bilden Sie dann die passenden Fragen und achten Sie dabei auf die Zeiten.

1. I'm going to look for my dog.

2. My friend is going to help me look.

3. I've found my dog's toy!

4. I will never give up looking!

5. If I were a dog, I would go to the park.

6. You should try looking in the park.

PRESENT PROGRESSIVE

1. *Where are you going?*

GOING TO-FUTURE

2. ______

PRESENT PERFECT

3. ______

WILL-FUTURE

4. ______

KONDITIONAL (INFINITIV)

5. ______

MODALVERB

6. ______

4. Schilderwald

Diese Schilder sagen Ihnen, was Sie tun und nicht tun sollten, aber nicht alle verwenden dafür einen Imperativ. Kreuzen Sie diejenigen Bilder an, bei denen das Verb in der Befehlsform steht.

1

2

3

4

5

6

7

8

5. Höflich, aber bestimmt

Mit dem Imperativ und *please* können Sie höfliche Bitten formulieren. Wandeln Sie die Sätze, wie im Beispiel, um.

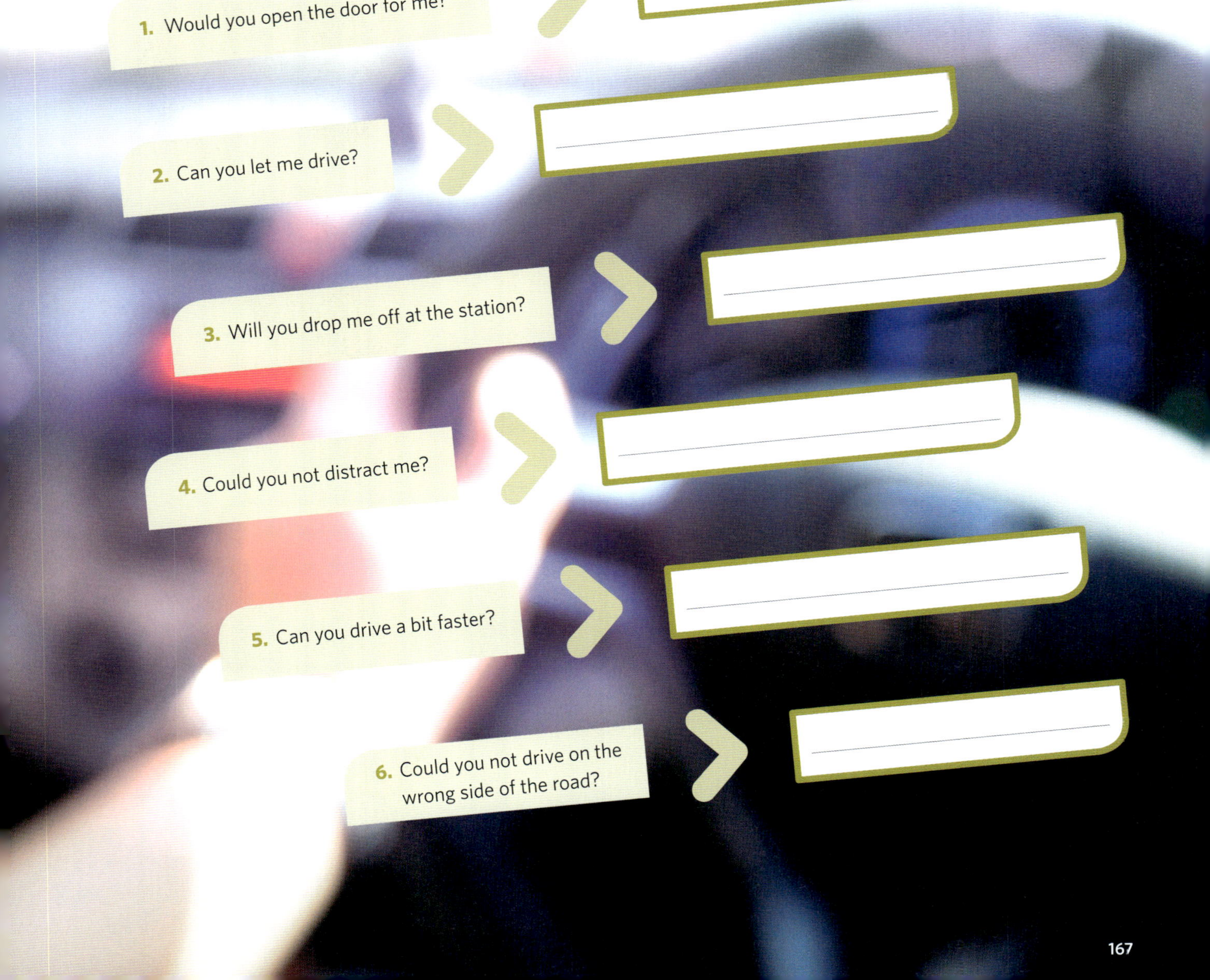

1. Would you open the door for me? > Open the door for me, please.
2. Can you let me drive? > ______
3. Will you drop me off at the station? > ______
4. Could you not distract me?
5. Can you drive a bit faster? > ______
6. Could you not drive on the wrong side of the road? > ______

Adverbiale Nebensätze können, wie Adverbien, die Umstände anderer Sätze näher bestimmen – und zwar zeitlich, kausal und modal. Meistens findet sich in einem adverbialen Nebensatz vor dem Subjekt eine Konjunktion.

6. Der richtige Zeitpunkt

Sylvie hat es schwer erwischt! Lesen Sie die Aussagen und bestimmen Sie, welche Funktion die Zeitadverbien in den adverbialen Nebensätzen erfüllen. Schreiben Sie sie in die passenden Boxen.

1. Verbinden von zwei Ereignissen

when ______ ______

2. Bezug auf ein nachfolgendes Ereignis

after ______

3. Bezug auf die Dauer zwischen zwei Zeitpunkten

______

4. Bezug auf etwas, das immer stattfindet

______

5. Bezug auf ein vorangehendes Ereignis

______

7. Genau darum!

Auch hier geht es romantisch zu. Leider fehlen in den adverbialen Nebensätzen die Adverbien zur kausalen Bestimmung. Setzen Sie sie in die richtigen Lücken ein, damit wir erfahren, warum was geschah.

given that

because

in view of

as

since

1

She was writing the romantic novel ________ she wanted an escape.

2

________ her recent break up, she needed to express herself.

3

She was excited ________ the novel was based on her own experience.

4

________ she had plenty of ideas, writing came naturally.

5

________ of the steamy content, she got a little embarrassed.

8. Ein guter Fang

Aus den durcheinandergeratenen Wörtern unten können Sie verschiedene Konditionalsätze bilden. Bringen Sie die Wörter in die richtige Reihenfolge und schreiben Sie die Sätze auf der nächsten Seite auf.

Mit **Konditionalsätzen** können Sie im Englischen Bedingungen formulieren. Sie werden wie Aussagesätze gebildet und meistens mit *if* eingeleitet. Sie können damit reale und irreale Bedingungen wiedergeben.

Bedingung **Ergebnis**

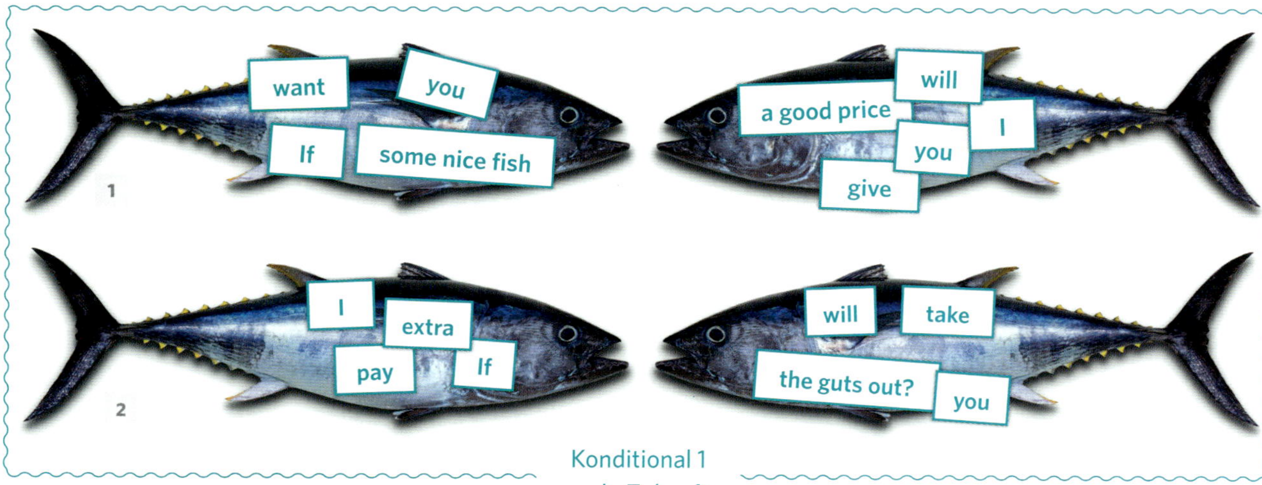

Konditional 1
reale Zukunft

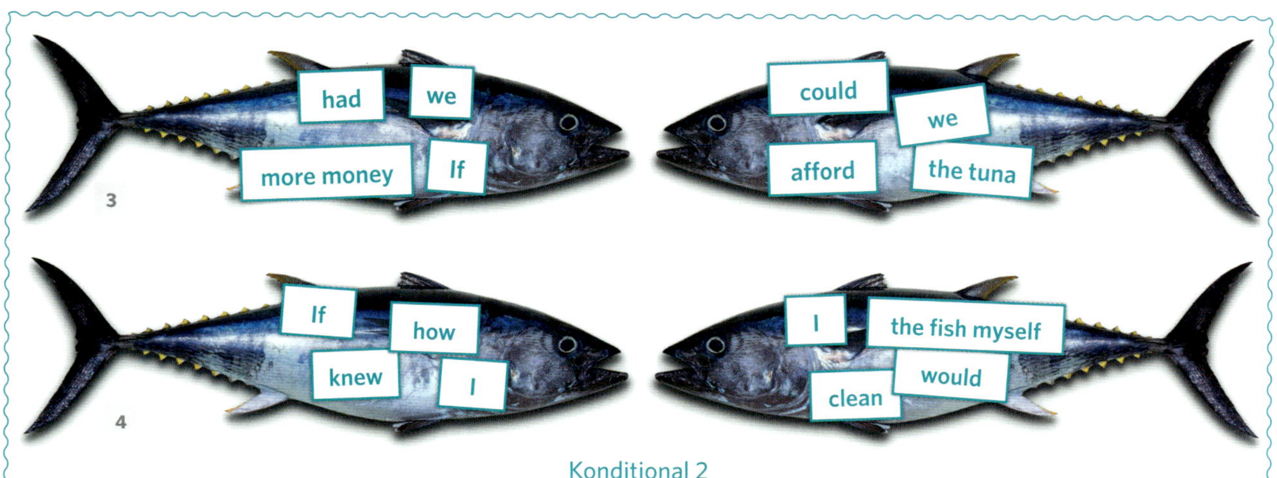

Konditional 2
irreale Zukunft

Bedingung Ergebnis

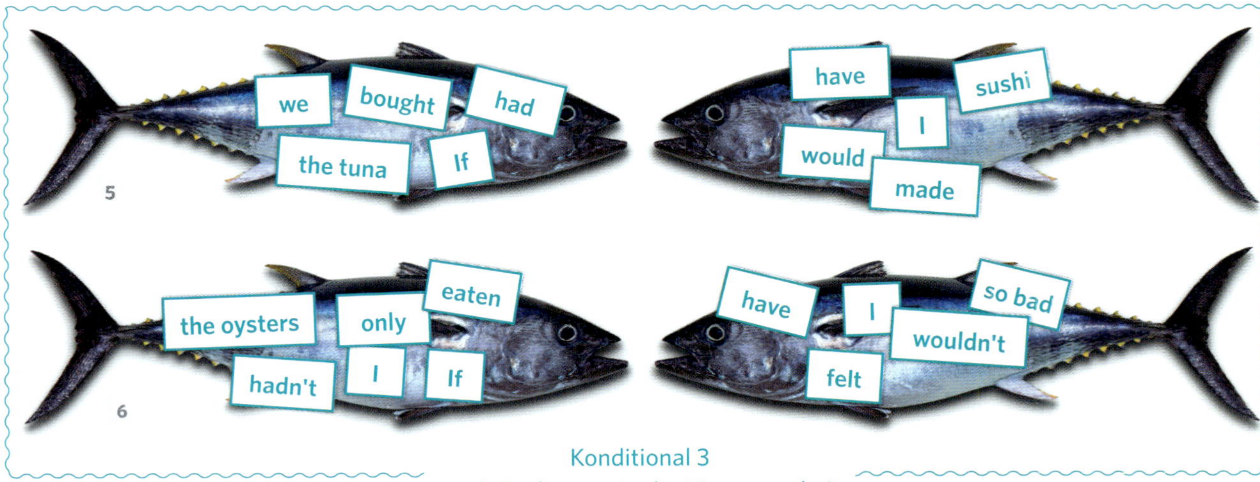

Konditional 3
ireale Bedingung in der Vergangenheit

1. *If you want some nice fish*, *I will give you a good price.*

2. ______________________, ______________________

3. ______________________, ______________________

4. ______________________, ______________________

5. ______________________, ______________________

6. ______________________, ______________________

Mit **Relativsätzen** können Sie ein Element eines Satzes, meistens das Substantiv, näher beschreiben. Relativsätze können sich aber auch auf das Objekt des Satzes beziehen. Achtung: in diesem Fall ändert sich die übliche Satzstellung (Subjekt - Verb - Objekt) zu Objekt - Subjekt - Verb. Relativpronomen nehmen dann den ersten Platz im Nebensatz ein.

9. Relativsätze

Lesen Sie die folgenden Relativsätze durch und beantworten Sie anschließend die Fragen auf der nächsten Seite.

1. non-defining

In the dead of night, when evil spirits do their work, nobody is safe.

2.

This is the only place ______ nobody can find us.

3.

The museum ______ holds many secrets is heavily guarded.

4.

He's the only person ______ knows the code.

Es gibt 2 Arten von Relativsätzen! *Defining* und *non-defining relative clauses*. Bei ersteren wird kein Komma verwendet, bei letzteren schon. Erstere sind zur Beschreibung eines Subjekts oder Objekts notwendig, letztere enthalten lediglich zusätzliche Informationen.

Es gibt zahlreiche Relativpronomen (*who, whose, which, where, when …*) Das neutrale *that* wird oft in *defining relative-clauses* anstelle von *who* oder *which* eingesetzt.

5.

She's the one _______ we must protect.

6.

There are many people _______ lives are at risk.

7.

_______ they want is redemption.

A. Füllen Sie die blauen Lücken mit dem passenden Relativpronomen.

where | whose | who | what | which | who | when

B. Entscheiden Sie, ob es sich um *defining, non defining* oder *free relative clauses* handelt. Setzen Sie Kommas, wo notwendig.

C. In zwei Sätzen kann das Relativpronomen durch *that* ersetzt werden. In welchen? ☐ ☐

D. In zwei Sätzen kann das Relativpronomen weggelassen werden. In welchen? ☐ ☐

10. Welch ein Drama!

Bei den alten Griechen sind die richtigen Formen verloren gegangen. Entscheiden Sie: Ist hier ein Infinitivsatz oder ein *-ing*-Satz passend? Füllen Sie entsprechend die Lücken mit der korrekten Form.

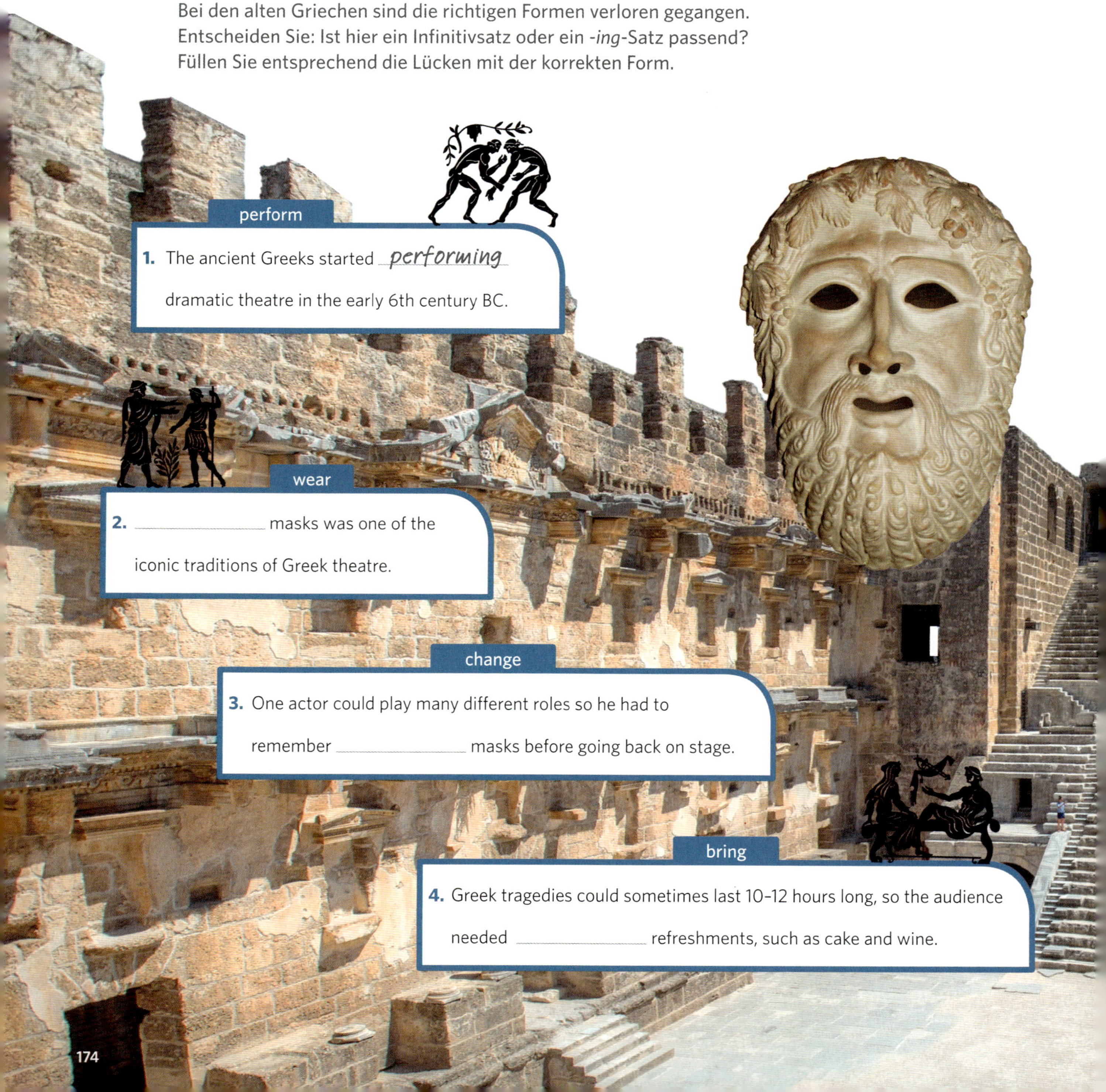

perform

1. The ancient Greeks started performing dramatic theatre in the early 6th century BC.

wear

2. ______ masks was one of the iconic traditions of Greek theatre.

change

3. One actor could play many different roles so he had to remember ______ masks before going back on stage.

bring

4. Greek tragedies could sometimes last 10–12 hours long, so the audience needed ______ refreshments, such as cake and wine.

Mit **Infinitivsätzen** (mit *to* oder *in order to*) kann man den Sinn und Zweck einer Handlung wiedergeben. Mit *-ing*-Sätzen, wenn sie vor einem Hauptsatz stehen, kann der Grund einer Handlung angegeben werden.

do

5. Actors were expected ________ outrageous things in order to get the audience's attention.

use

6. The actors involved the audience by ________ audience interaction and participation.

win

7. Greek playwrights even gave gifts to the audience because they wanted ________ their approval.

throw

8. If the audience didn't like the play, they enjoyed ________ food at the actors.

11. Was für eine Frage ...

Wenn Sie berichten möchten, was eine Person gesagt oder gefragt hat, verwenden Sie die indirekte Rede oder indirekte Fragesätze. Der indirekten Rede geht oft *that* voraus. Vor indirekten Fragen stehen oft *if*, *whether* (etwas formeller als *if*) oder Fragewörter (*who, where, when...*). Sie werden häufig von Verben wie *ask, wonder* oder *know* eingeleitet. Achtung bei der Zeitform des Verbs! Sie richtet sich nach der Zeitform im Hauptsatz.

Wandeln Sie die untenstehenden Interviewfragen in indirekte Fragen um.

1 Is the team ready for tomorrow's game?

2 What have you done in training this week?

3 Will you be playing the 4-4-2 system tomorrow?

4 Are you going to play the big man up front?

5 Did the players celebrate after last week's performance?

1. They asked him *if/whether the team was ready for tomorrow's game.*
2. They wondered ______
3. They wanted to know ______
4. They asked him ______
5. They wondered ______

12. Was hat er gesagt?

Wandeln Sie nun die direkte Rede in die indirekte Rede um. Achten Sie auf die Zeiten.

1 "The team is very prepared ahead of tomorrow's match."

5 "The players didn't celebrate last week – they can celebrate when they win the league!"

2 "We have practised defending because we don't want to conceed any goals."

3 "I am thinking about trying a new system tomorrow."

4 "The striker may play tomorrow, but I will decide later."

1. He stated that *the team is/was very prepared ahead of tomorrow's match.*

2. He said that ______________________________

3. He told reporters that ______________________________

4. He revealed that ______________________________

5. He said that ______________________________

16 Die Verneinung

Wie verneine ich im Englischen?

Welche Möglichkeiten habe ich hierfür?

1. ... oder auch nicht!

Lesen Sie die Sätze zu den Fotos und bilden Sie die verneinte Form, wie im Beispiel. Verwenden Sie Kurzformen.

1

\+ They **are** hungry because it **is** lunch time.

– They aren't hungry because it isn't lunch time.

2

\+ The joke **was** funny, so he **was** laughing.

– ______________________

3

\+ They **exercise** because it **makes** a difference.

– ______________________

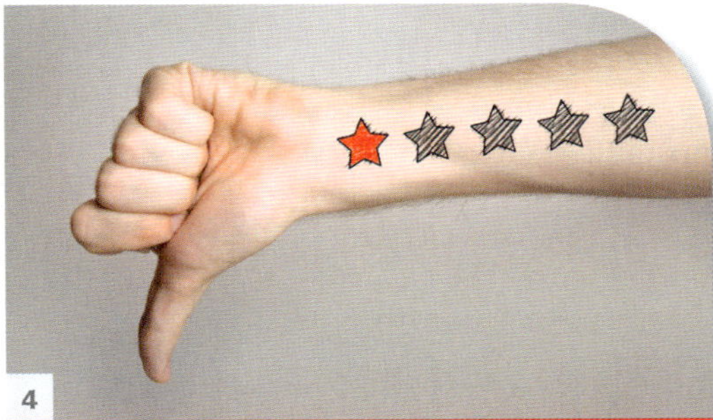

4

+ I **have seen** the film, which **got** good reviews.

– ______________________________

____

5

+ He **cleaned** the bathroom because she **had reminded** him.

– ______________________________

____

6

+ You **must** believe everything you read!

– ______________________________

____

7

+ I **can** do it and I sure as hell **will** do it!

– ______________________________

____

2. Eine Frage der Abstufung

Um im Englischen etwas zu verneinen, können Sie negative Adverbien wie *hardly (ever)*, *rarely* und *never* verwenden. Tragen Sie Sie in die Lücken ein, um das Diagramm zu beschreiben.

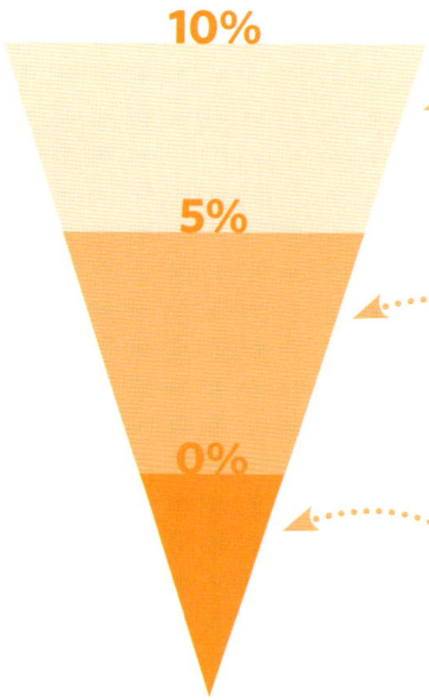

1. sehr selten = ______________
2. fast nie = ______________
3. überhaut nicht = ______________

3. Nie, selten oder kaum?

Schauen Sie sich das Beispiel an. Schreiben Sie dann, wie im Beispiel, die Sätze auf der nächsten Seite so um, dass sie eine möglichst ähnliche Bedeutung wiedergeben. Verwenden Sie dabei *hardly (ever)*, *rarely* und *never*. Achtung! Dabei benötigen Sie nicht mehr *do* als Hauptverb und das negative Adverb ersetzt *not*.

I only buy new clothes once a year.

1. *I hardly ever buy new clothes.*

I don't miss any fashion sales.

2.

I don't go out much.

3.

I only stay in when I'm ill.

4.

I don't ever meet new people.

5.

I don't often miss the chance to meet new people.

6.

4. *No*

Wenn Sie nicht das Verb, sondern beispielsweise Substantive verneinen möchten, geht dies am einfachsten mit dem Negativpartikel *no*. Aus *no* wird in Kombination auch *nobody, nothing* und *nowhere*.

Tim erzählt von seiner Reise – füllen Sie die Lücken mit *no, nobody, nothing* und *nowhere*. Einmal müssen Sie *never* einsetzen.

5. *Any*

Verneinungen können auch mit *not + any* formuliert werden. Hierfür benötigt man die verneinte Form von *do* in der passenden Zeitform. Tim erzählt erneut von seiner Reise. Diesmal verwendet er *not + any*. Schauen Sie sich das Beispiel an und schreiben Sie die Sätze aus Übung 4 um, indem Sie vorgehen wie im Beispiel. Verwenden Sie die angegebenen Verneinungen.

1. *I didn't have any hobbies.*

2. ______________________________

3. ______________________________

4. ______________________________

5. ______________________________

6. ______________________________

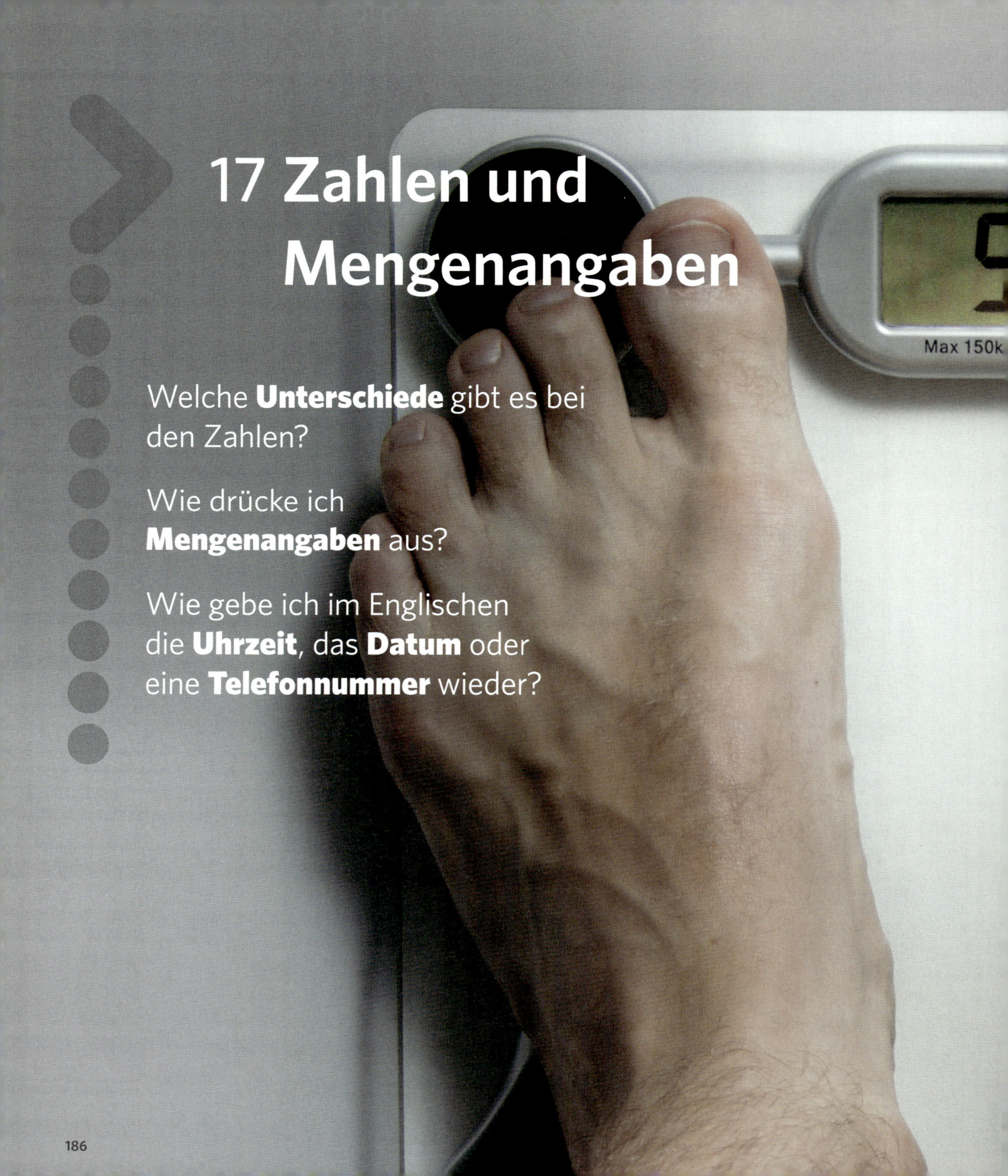

17 Zahlen und Mengenangaben

Welche **Unterschiede** gibt es bei den Zahlen?

Wie drücke ich **Mengenangaben** aus?

Wie gebe ich im Englischen die **Uhrzeit**, das **Datum** oder eine **Telefonnummer** wieder?

kg
kg d=100g

1. Kardinalzahlen

Schreiben Sie die Zahlen, die Sie auf den Bildern sehen, aus.

1. twenty-eight

2. ______________________

3. ______________________

4. ______________________

5. ______________________

6. ______________________

7. ______________________

2. Nur nicht konkret werden

Wenn Sie keine genauen Zahlen nennen möchten oder können, helfen Ihnen die unten angegebenen Ausdrücke eine ungefähre Menge zu beschreiben. Manche geben auch die konkrete Anzahl in anderen Worten wieder. Setzen Sie die passenden Begriffe ein.

1 a pair of ducks

a dozen	beers
She's in her	pancakes
a few	eggs
about 250	of ducks
thirty or so	sixties
~~a pair~~	millilitres

2

3

4

5

6

3. Erster!

In der Wortschlange haben sich Ordinalzahlen versteckt. Suchen Sie sie und tragen Sie ihre gekürzten Formen in die passenden Stufen ein. Denken Sie daran: 1., 2. und 3. sind unregelmäßig!

4. Besondere Termine

Diese wichtigen Tage sollte man nicht vergessen. Schreiben Sie das jeweilige Datum mit gekürzter Ordinalzahl aus. Nicht vergessen: das *the* wird zwar immer mitgesprochen, aber nie ausgeschrieben (*1st January = the first of January*).

1. New Year's Day is on 1st January.

2. Valentine's Day is on ______________.

3. St. Patrick's Day is on ______________.

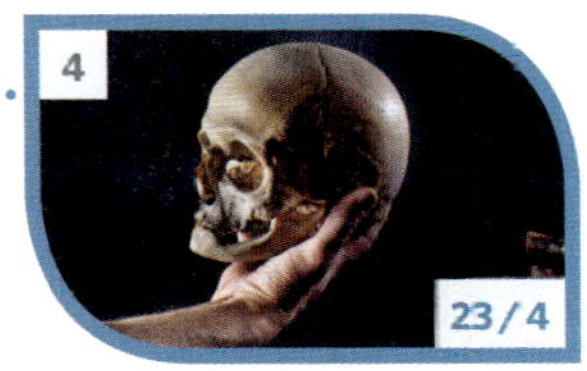

4. Shakespeare's Day is on ______________.

5. Coconut Day is on ______________.

6. Halloween is on ______________.

7. Christmas Day is on ______________.

5. Lange ist es her

Tragen Sie die passenden Jahreszahlen in den Zeitstrahl ein – beginnend ganz früher bis in die heutige Zeit. Schreiben Sie die Zahlen dann aus.

99 AD | 59 BC | 1966 | 1138 | 1703 | ~~401 BC~~ | ~~2015~~ | 1986

401 BC

1. four hundred and one BC

2. ______________________

3. ______________________

4. ______________________

5. ______________________

6. ______________________

7. ______________________

2015

8. ______________________

6. Dezimalzahlen

Schreiben Sie die ausgeschriebenen Zahlen als Nummern mit den korrekten Dezimaltrennzeichen. Achtung: Wo im Deutschen ein Komma zur Trennung steht, steht im Englischen immer ein Punkt – und andersherum!

1 Zero point zero two > ______

2 Five point nine six > ______

3 Thirteen pounds and twenty three pence > ______

4 Nineteen point zero four seven > ______

5 Four hundred and forty four pounds fifty five pence > ______

6 Thirteen thousand and twelve point seven eight > ______

7. In die Brüche gegangen

Im Englischen werden besonders häufig die Brüche *half, quarter, third* und *fifth* verwendet. Achtung: *half* steht ohne Artikel direkt vor dem Substantiv. Bei allen anderen Brüchen benötigt man *a* bzw. *the* und *of* vor dem Substantiv. Tragen Sie unten die passenden Brüche ein.

1

Half a lemon.

2

Three ________ of an hour.

3

One ________ of a doughnut.

4

A ________ of a pizza.

5

An ________ of a melon.

6

A ________ of a cake.

quarters

sixth

~~half~~

third

fourteenth

eighth

8. So geht es kürzer

Schreiben Sie nun die Brüche in numerischer Form.

1 $\frac{1}{2}$

2 ——

3 ——

4 ——

5 ——

6 ——

9. Aus eins mach mehr

Wenn Sie Zahlen vervielfältigen möchten, verwenden Sie in der Regel *times* (fünf Mal = *five times*). Für **doppelt, dreifach** und **vierfach** gibt es auch Sonderwörter: *double/twice, triple, quadruple*. Sie können aber auch mit *times* vervielfältigt werden.

Betrachten Sie die Bilder und Texte. Verbinden Sie die passenden Paare und befüllen Sie die Lücken.

three times · once · triple · twenty-eight times · double · quadrupled

A

B

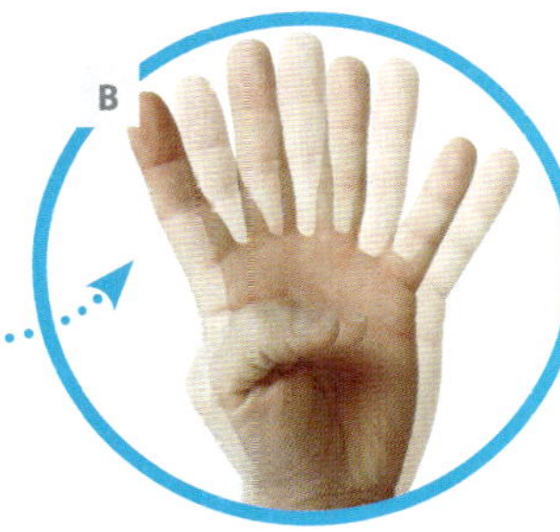

C

D

E

F

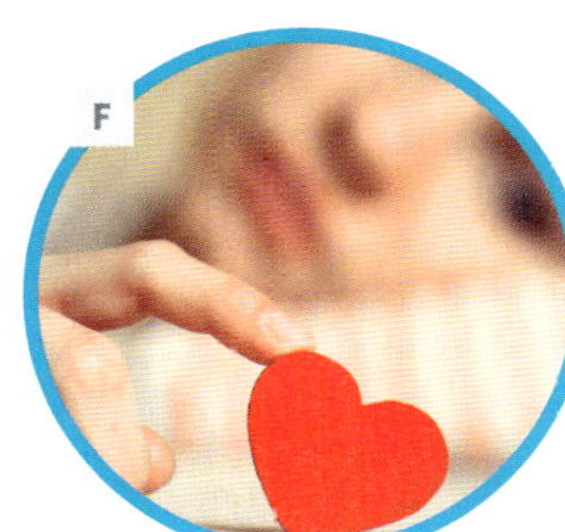

1. I think I'm seeing _double_.
2. That's a ________ -decker sandwich.
3. I have ________ as many emails as I did this morning!
4. He had to write the same thing ________________.
5. True love only happens ________ in a lifetime.
6. I only asked for two scoops. You've ________ my order!

10. Wieviel Uhr ist es?

Geben Sie die Uhrzeiten an, die Sie unten sehen. Schreiben Sie die Uhrzeiten dabei aus wie im Beispiel. Denken Sie daran, im Englischen wird fast ausschließlich die 12-Stunden-Zählung verwendet. Ab der halben Stunde sagen Sie für die verbleibenden Minuten bis zur vollen Stunde *to* (17:50 Uhr = *ten to six*).

1. Half past two.

2. ______________________

3. ______________________

4. ______________________

5. ______________________

6. ______________________

11. *am* oder *pm?*

Aufgrund der 12-Stunden-Zählung wird mit *am* und *pm* (lat. ante/post meridiem – vor/nach dem Mittag) angegeben, um welche Uhrzeit es sich handelt.
Tragen Sie die Uhrzeiten aus Übung 10 nun an der richtigen Stelle ein.
Verwenden Sie die numerische Form. Stunde und Minute werden durch : getrennt.

12. Zählbar oder nicht zählbar?

Manche Dinge können Sie zählen, manche nicht (z.B. Flüssigkeiten). Entsprechend werden unterschiedliche Mengenangaben benutzt, um nähere Angaben zu machen. Sie sehen sie in den kleinen Kästchen. Tragen Sie die Mengenangaben ein, von der größten Menge hin zur geringsten.

countable

1. lots of / a lot of
2. ______________________
3. ______________________
4. ______________________

uncountable

5. ______________________
6. ______________________
7. ______________________
8. ______________________
9. ______________________

13. Ist noch was übrig?

Verwenden Sie nun einige der Mengenangaben aus Übung 12 um die Fragen und Antworten unten zu vervollständigen. Nicht vergessen! Mit *how many* wird nach zählbaren und mit *how much* nach unzählbaren Substantiven gefragt.

1. How ______ bottles of wine have we got left?

We've got ______ bottles!

2. How ______ cheese is there in the fridge?

There's a ______, but we should buy some more.

3. How ______ grapes shall I buy?

Buy a ______ of grapes to go with the cheese!

4. How ______ ham is there?

There's not ______, you'd better get some more.

Lösungen

Lösungen

Kapitel 1

1. 1. the, a; 2. a; 3. a, the, 4. a; 5. The; 6. a/-; 7. The; 8. the; 9. -; 10: the, -
2. 1. an actor, 2. a dog, 3. a bicycle, 4. an ear, 5. a pen, 6. an eagle, 7. an umbrella, 8. a teacher, 9. an orange, 10. a car, 11. a helicopter, 12. a cat, 13. an ambulance, 14. a calendar, 15. an egg, 16. a spoon

Kapitel 2

1. 1. B June, 2. E Italy, 3. A Friday, 4. D Thanksgiving, 5. C Spanish, 6. F Madame Tussaud's
2. 1. Ms, 2. Prof, 3. Dr, 4. Mr, 5. Mrs
3. 1. foxes, 2. sandwiches, 3. boys, 4. wolves, 5. strawberries, 6. glasses
4. **ZÄHLBAR:** table, magazines, tablet, pen, newspapers, horse; **NICHT ZÄHLBAR:** apple juice, bread, coffee, sugar, money, rice
5. 1. glasses, 2. trousers, 3. scissors, 4. jeans, 5. clothes, 6. stairs
6. 1. She, 2. He, 3. it, 4. she, 5. it 6. He
7. 2. Jason is Tom's friend. **He**'s a nurse/doctor. 3. Here's my husband. **He**'s a (math) teacher. 4. And this is Tom's wife. **She**'s a pilot.
8. 1. Kate's motorbike, 2. Tom's cat, 3. parents' car, 4. Charles' birthday cake, 5. children's toys, 6. girls' phones (*auch:* smartphones/mobile phones/mobiles)
9. 1. name of the school, 2. tourist industry of Spain, 3. history of London, 4. top floor of the building

Kapitel 3

1. 1. She (SU), 2. it (OP), 3. them (OP), 4. He (SP), 5. her (OP), 6. They (SP)
2. 1. his, 2. your, 3. my, 4. their, 5. her, 6. yours, 7. Mine, 8. our
3. **waagerecht:** 2. ourselves, 5. herself, 6. myself, 8. themselves; **senkrecht:** 1. yourselves, 3. itself, 4. yourself, 7. himself
4. 1. This, 2. That, 3. Those, 4. These
5. 1. One, one, 2. People, they, 3. You, you, 4. he/she, he/she
6. A 5, B 8, C 7, D 6, E 3, F 2, G 1, H 4

Kapitel 4

1. 1. in, 2. at, 3. In, 4. on, 5. during, 6. until, 7. at/around, 8. for, 9. Since
2. 1. on, 2. in, 3. under, 4. in front of, 5. over. 6. by/next to, 7. against, 8. behind, 9. next to
3. 2. above, 3. next to, 4. against, 5. in, 6. in front of, 7. under
4. 2. onto, 3. along, 4. over, 5. through, 6. into
5. 2. to, 3. of, 4. for, 5. to, 6. of

Kapitel 5

1. **passende Bilder/Adjektive:** 2. F, 3. B, 4. D, 5. E, 6. C, 7. I, 8. G, 9. H, **Gegenteile:** tall/short, hungry/full, active/lazy, happy/sad, hard,diffcult/easy, long/short, old/young, old/new
2. **-ful:** peaceful, careful, useful, **-al:** cultural, national, seasonal, **-ous:** adventurous, famous, dangerous, **-able:** acceptable, comfortable, reasonable, **-ive:** active, defensive, expensive, **-ish:** foolish, childish, selfish, **-less:** useless, endless, heartless, selfless, **-ly:** friendly, woolly, deadly, **-y:** stormy, windy, cloudy,
3. 1. sleeping/crying, 2. bored/pouring, 3. lost/falling, 4. winning/signed
4. 2. American, 3. Swiss, 4. Thai, 5. French, 6. Japanese
5. tall, tallest, the tallest; short, shorter, the shortest; big, bigger, the biggest; thin, thinner, the thinnest; large, larger, the largest; nice, nicer, the nicest; funny, funnier, the funniest; lazy, lazier, the laziest; pretty, prettier, the prettiest; dangerous, more dangerous, the most dangerous; comfortable, more comfortable, the most comfortable; **unregelmäßige Adjektive:** good, better, the best; bad, worse, the worst; far, further/farther, the furthest/farthest
6. 2. shorter, 3. bigger, 4. thinner, 5. the nicest, 6. the funniest, 7. lazier, 8. the prettiest, 9. the most dangerous
7. 2. smaller than, 3. is not as big as the African Elephant, 4. as heavy as, 5. the most poisonous, 6. not as poisonous as the snail, 7. nearly as dangerous as
8. 2. an active, young woman, 3. a warm, woolly jumper, 4. a famous, old statue, 5. a cold, windy day, 6. an expensive watch
9. 1. early, 2. ready, 3. beautiful, 4. nervous, 5. excited, 6. pouring, 7. wet, 8. handsome, 9. luckiest, 10. delicious, 11. good, 12. drunk

Kapitel 6

1. **Adjektive:** 1. slow, 3. slow, 5. slowest, **Adverbien:** 2. slowly, 3. really, 4. extremely, slowly, 5. Actually. Sätze in der richtigen Reihenfolge: 1. Sloths are slow. 2. Sloths move slowly. 3. Sloths are really slow creatures. 4. Sloths move extremely slowly. 5. Actually, sloths are the slowest creatures in the jungle. (*auch:* Actually, the slowest creatures in the jungle are sloths.)
2. 1. quietly, 2. normally, 3. carefully, 4. happily, 5. probably, 6. cheekily
3. **Adjektive:** 1. back, 2. deep, 3. high, 4. hard, 5. fast, 6. lovely, **Adverbien:** 1. left, 2. late, 3. hard, 4. wrong, 5. hardly, 6. nearly
4. 1. more beautifully, the most beautifully; 2. more quickly, the most quickly; 3. later, the latest; 4. higher, the highest;

5. better, the best;
6. worse, the worst

5. 1. worst, 2. as/as, 3. more, 4. better, 5. as/as

6. 1. terribly, 2. never, 3. very, 4. always, 5. today, 6. wildly, 7. hardly, 8. quickly, 9. usually; A terribly, B never, C very, D always, E Today, F wildly, G hardly, H quickly, I usually

Kapitel 7

1. 1. both, 2. although, 3. so, 4. until, 5. neither, 6. but, 7. and, 8. so that, 9. because

Kapitel 8

1. **REGELMÄSSIGE VERBEN:** love, live, smile, work; **UNREGELMÄSSIGE VERBEN (Grundform, Past Simple, Past Participle)** sleep ,slept, slept; take, took, taken; buy, bought, bought; do, did, done; make, made, made; learn, learnt, learnt

2. **TRANSITIV:** 4., 6., **INTRANSITIV:** 2., 5., **REFLEXIV:** 1., 3.

3. 1. (was)/'m, 2. were, 're, 3. was, 's, 4. were, 're

4. 1. She **is** meeting new people. 2. **Is** she forgetting about him? 3. She **is** kissed by a stranger. 4. She **has** left her old life behind. 5. They **haven't** seen each other since. 6. What if he **had** made more effort?

5. 1. **Does** the bed feel comfortable? 2. No, I **didn't** sleep well. 3. **Do** you like eggs? 4. I **don't** eat dairy products.

6. 1. **I'll** get up soon. 2. The day **won't** last forever. 3. **Will** you make me breakfast in bed? 4. I'**ll** make you lunch in bed!

7 **TRUE:** 1, 4., 6. **FALSE:** 2. 3, 5.

8. **Vorschlag:** 1. **Erlaubnis:** 2., 3. **Aufforderung/Befehl:** 6. **Sonstige Fragen:** 4., 5.

9. 1. to look **after** sb/sth – sich um jdn./etw. kümmern, 2. to look **forward** to sth – *sich auf etw. freuen,* 3. to look **up** sb/sth – (an jdm./etw.) hochschauen, 4. to look **through** sb/sth – jdn./etw. durchsehen, 5. to look **at** ab/sth – jdn./etw. betrachten, 6. to look **for** sb/sth – nach jdm./etw. suchen

10. 2. look forward to, 3. look at, 4. look for, 5. look through, look - up

11 1. Be, 2. Let's, 3. Don't, 4. Help – please, 5. Let's not, 6. Help - please

12. 2. The factory was built in 1991. 3. The cakes can be smelled/smelt by everyone in town. 4. 11,000 cakes are produced a day. 5. A secret recipe for cupcakes was invented by Mr Sprinkles. 6. The secret recipe must not be given to anyone.

13. 1. going, 2. jumping, 3. slaloming, 4. hitting, 5. feeling, 6. using, 7. snowboarding, 8. looking, 9. relaxing

14. 2. Tom wants to take Sue on a date. 3. Sue suggests going for dinner. 4. Sue imagines being treated like a princess, 5. Sue agrees to date him. 6. Sue expects him to pay!

15. 1. B, 2. E, 3. A, 4. C, 5. D, 6. H, 7. F, 8. G

Kapitel 9

1. 1. Tony Hill is..., 2. He is thinking..., 3. He has completed..., 4. He has been running..., 5. He broke.... 6. My heart was hurting..., 7. I had not experienced..., 8. Tony had been running..., 9. I will run..., 10. I will be running..., 11. He will have set..., 12. He will have been running...

Kapitel 10

1. 1. walked, 2. started, 3. destroyed, 4. tried, 5. stopped, 6. needed, 7. copied, 8. kissed, 9. hated

2. **[d]** destroyed, tried, copied, **[t]** walked, stopped, kissed, **[id]** started, needed, hated

3. 2. catch – caught, 3. drink – drank, 4. forget - forgot, 5. go – went, 6. hear – heard, 7. read – read, *auch:* learn – learnt, 8. bake - baked, 9. see – saw, 10. teach – taught, *auch:* learn - learnt

4. 1. Did, 2. didn't, 3. Did, 4. did, 5. didn't

5. 1. ...when I was a little boy., 2. When I was a student..., 3. ...5 minutes ago., 4. ...a long time ago.. 5. ...yesterday?, 6. ...last summer...

6. 2. She was watching TV. (*oder:* She wasn't doing anything.) 3. He was going/travelling to work. 4. She was sleeping. 5. She was eating/having breakfast. 6. He wasn't working/ He was relaxing. 7. He was cooking/ making dinner. 8. She was relaxing. 9. She was eating fruit.

7. 1. was snowing, was walking / Funktion: Beschreibung der Szene und Hintergrundhandlungen, 2. was thinking / Funktion: vorübergehende Handlung, 3. were sitting/watching / Funktion: eine Handlung zu einer bestimmten Zeit, 4. were not doing, was working / Funktion: zwei Handlungen, die gleichzeitig ablaufen, 5. were collecting / Funktion: nach *while,* 6. were building / Funktion: Betonung der Dauer, 7. were sleeping / Funktion: eine Handlung zu einer bestimmten Zeit

8. 2. heard, was thinking, 3. were, were getting, 4. was walking, saw, 5. was crying, met, 6. was dreaming, was beating, began, 7. were...doing, saw, were...playing, was...holding

9. 2. had...seen, 3. hadn't, 4. had...left, 5. had, 6. had...put, 7. had put, 8. had forgotten

10. 2. He cycled to the park. 3. He arrived at the park. 4. He realised he had forgotten his key. 5. He put his bike near the pond. 6. He went to get an ice-cream. 7. Someone stole the bike.

11. 2. had been knitting, 3. had been chewing, 4. had been arguing, 5. had not been expecting

12. 1. had been waiting, arrived, 2. had been cutting, broke, 3. had finished, rang, 4. had eaten, washed up, began

13. 1. had been looking, found, 2. met, had been living, 3. was looking, found, 4. married, were living

14. 2. haven't, 3. has, 4. Hasn't, 5. hasn't

15. 2. caught, 3. driven, 4. forgotten, 5. gone, 6. known, 7. made, 8. seen

16. 2. caught, so far, 3. never, driven, 4. ever, forgotten, 5. just, gone, 6. known, for, 7. made, yet, 8. seen, already

17. 1. worked, 2. stayed, 3. have worked, 4. have eaten, 5. have tried

18. 1. have worked, 2. got, 3. studied, 4. have had, 5. has reviewed

19. 2. He has been exercising. 3. They have been drinking. 4. They have not been listening.

20. 2. Has he been doing yoga? No he hasn't. 3. Have they been studying? No they haven't. 4. Have they been climbing? Yes they have.

21. 2. He's been learning Japanese for 6 months. 3. He's been working as an English teacher for 3 months. 4. He's been meeting a lot of new people lately. 5. He's been looking forward to going out all week. 6. He's been singing karaoke all night.

22. 2. A (present perfect progressive), 3. D (present progressive), 4. C (present perfect progressive)

23. 2. D (present perfect progressive), 3. C (present perfect), 4. A (present perfect progressive)

Kapitel 11

1. 1. live, 2. love, 3. are not/aren't, 4. enjoys, 5. dresses, 6. goes, 7. does, 8. has, 9. can

2. 1. Does, do, 2. doesn't, 3. doesn't, 4. Don't, 5. Do, 6. don't

3. 1. every weekend (regelmäßiges Ereignis), 2. in a few days (geplante Ereignisse in der Zukunft), 3. always (regelmäßiges Ereignis), 4. usually (regelmäßiges Ereignis), 5. If (Konditional *(if + present simple)*)

4. 2. They're fighting. - They're not fighting. - Are they fighting?, 3. He's balancing. - He's not balancing. - Is he balancing?, 4. He's getting angry. - He's not getting angry. - Is he getting angry?, 5. He's hanging. - He's not hanging. - Is he hanging?

5. 2. right now (Ereignisse, die im Moment des Sprechens stattfinden), 3. at the moment (Ereignisse, die im Moment des Sprechens stattfinden), 4. tomorrow (geplante Ereignisse), 5. always (regelmäßige Ereignisse), 6. this evening (geplante Ereignisse)

6. 2. D, 3. G, 4. F, 5. A, 6. E, 7. C

Kapitel 12

1. 2. She's going to cook fish and chips. 3. Is she going to run on Sunday afternoon? 4. She's not going to do anything. 5. She's going to buy fresh fish. 6. She's going to eat a roast dinner.

2. 2. She's going to be eating a roast dinner., 3. She's going to be running in the park.

3. 2. She's not going to be eating roast dinner/ Is she going to be eating roast dinner? 3. She's not going to be running in the park/ Is she going to be running in the park?

4. 2. wrap up warm, 3. put on suncream, 4. wear wellies, 5. wear sunglasses, 6. take a scarf and gloves

5. 2. It's going to be snowing. 3. It's not going to be raining, the sun is going to be shining. 4. I'm going to take an umbrella and wear wellies. 4. I'm going to wrap up warm and take a scarf and gloves.6. I'm going to put on suncream and wear sunglasses.

6. 1. Will, will, 'll; 2. Will, will, 'll, 3. Will, won't, won't

7. 2. In two hours it'll be walking in the forest. 3. This time tomorrow they'll be swimming in the sea. 4. On Sunday afternoon I'll be playing football with my son.

8. 2. ...will be successful. (Verwendung im Konditionalsatz mit *if*), 3. ...will never get out of it alive. (Versprechen), 4. ...will be famous for 15 minutes. (Vorhersagen/ Tatsachen in der Zukunft), 5. ...will never be content. (Verwendung im Konditionalsatz mit *if*), 6. ...will be sunshine. (Vorhersagen/Tatsachen in der Zukunft), 7. ...will never reach your destination, ... (Verwendung im Konditionalsatz mit *if*)

9. 2. Our plane takes off at 13.00. 3. We're arriving in Johannesburg at 18.00. 4. We're taking a taxi to the hotel at 19.00. 5. We're having dinner at 21.00. 6. We're waking up at 7.00. 7. The bus leaves at 9.00. 8, The safari starts at 19.30. 9. We're having a meeting at 18.00. 10. We're going to a photo sharing session at 21.00.

10. 2. He will have had breakfast. 3. They won't have gone to bed. 4. Will he have gone for a run?

11. 2. He will have been working for 2 hours, 3. They will have been sleeping for an hour, 4. Will he have been running for 5 minutes?

12. 2. noch im Gange, 3. noch im Gange, 4. abgeschlossen, 5. abgeschlossen, 6. noch im Gange, 7. abgeschlossen, 8. abgeschlossen.

13. 2. Vorhersage, 3. Entscheidung, 4. Plan/Absicht, 5. Versprechen

14. 2. Vorhersage, 3. Plan/Absicht, 4. Vorhersage, 5. Entscheidung, 6. Versprechen

15. 2. Shall we go out for dinner? 3. Shall I clean it? 4. You shall obey me! 5. Shall we do something?

16. 2. ...will you do the washing up? 3. ...we'll order a takeaway., 4. ...I'll just make myself a salad. 5. you'll have to make me dinner.

17. 2. it will be, 3. we are going to win, 4. we won't do

18. 2. it would be, 3. we were going to win, 4. we wouldn't do

Kapitel 13

1. 2. I wouldn't be happy. 3. She'd make some soup. 4. He wouldn't get to work. 5. He'd build an igloo. 6. We wouldn't have to go to school.

2. 2. Wouldn't we go sledging? 3. Would we build a snowman? 4. Wouldn't we build a snowman?

3. 2. ...if you came with me. 3 ...if I had a car. 4. ...if I didn't have to work. 5....but I don't have time. 6. ...but I don't feel like partying.

4. 1. A, 2. C, 3. D, 4. B

5. 2. ...we'd be thinking about moving house. 3. ...he wouldn't be climbing it. 4. ...he wouldn't be feeling so relaxed. 5. ...would they be taking a tour? 6. would they be looking into the crater?

6. 1. A, 2. C, 3. B, 4. would, 5. could, 6. might

7. 2. I could buy that car. 3. I could cruise with the top down. 4. I might be driving it now.

8. 2. I would have made the interview. 3. I would/might not have overslept. 4. I would/might not have missed my chance. 5. Would/Could I have got the job? 6. Would/Could I have been a success?

9. 2. ... if I hadn't gone to the club. 3. ...if I had remembered the interview. 4. ...if my team had won the match. 5. ...but I got too excited. 6. ...but Dom made me do shots.

10. 2. ...she would have been getting nice and brown. 3. ...she would not have been feeling miserable. 4. ... she would not have been booking another holiday. 5. ...wouldn't she have been enjoying herself? 6. would she have been dancing with a stranger?

11. 2. E, 3. C, 4. D, 5. F, 6. A; hypothetische Zukunft: 1. B, 3. C, 5. F, hypothetische Vergangenheit: 2. E, 4. D, 6. A

12. 2. If I could have gone anywhere, I'd have gone to Peru. 3. If I could take anybody with me, I'd take you. 4. If I could have taken anybody with me, I'd have taken you. 5. Would you come with me if I asked you to come? 6. Would you have come with me if I'd asked you to come?

Kapitel 14

1. 1. Humans (S) discovered (V) fire (O). 2. Fire (S) produces (V) heat and light (O). 3. We (S) use (V) fire (O) for many different reasons (E/N). 4. Controlling fire (S) was (V) an important step (O) for early humans (E/N). 5. They (S) could cook (V) food (O) for themselves (E/N). 6. They (S) were able to scare away (V) dangerous animals (O). 7. Archaeologists (S) have found (V) evidence of fire (O) from 700,000 years ago (E/N).

2. 2. Uncle Tony did the cooking because he fancies himself as a chef. 3. My auntie made everyone cocktails. 4. Even though some of the sausages were burnt, it was still a nice afternoon.

3. **Subjekt:** you, who, auntie, anyone, **Verb:** did, eat, burnt, did, put, is, **Objekt**: How many sausages, the sausages, How much vodka, **Ergänzung/Nebensatz:** still hungry, in the cocktails

4. 1. A full stop is used at the end of a sentence. To be a sentence it must have a complete clause. 2. There are two main rules about using colons: ... 3. B, 4. Parenthesis (sometimes called brackets) are used to... 5. "We use quotation marks to present direct speech or an exact quote," my teacher said. 6. B

5. ...at work, / ...more tired, / In fact, ... / ...of the road, / Nevertheless, ...

Kapitel 15

1. 3. Does the dog want a bone? 4. No, the dog doesn't want a bone. 5. Can you feed the dog? 6. Can you help me find the turtle? 7. Was the tank open? 8. Were the turtles inside? 9. Did the turtle escape? 10. Did you forget to close the tank?

2. 2. What, 3. Which, 4. Why, 5. Where, 6. When, 7. How

3. 2. Who is going to help you look? 3. What have you found? 4. When will you give up looking? 5. Where would you go if you were a dog? 6. What should I do?/Where should I look?

4. Imperativformen: 1., 4. 6. 7.

5. 2. Let me drive, please. 3. Drop me off at the station, please. 4. Don't distract me, please. 5. Drive a bit faster, please. 6. Don't drive on the wrong side of the road, please.

6. 1. when, as, while; 2. after, as soon as; 3. since; 4. whenever; 5. before

7. 1. as, 2. in view of, 3. since 4. given that, 5. because

8. 2. If I pay extra, will you take the guts out? 3. If we had more money, we could afford the tuna. 4. If I knew how, I would clean the fish myself 5. If we had bought the tuna, I would have made some sushi. 6. If only I hadn't eaten the oysters, I wouldn't have felt so bad.

9. **A:** 2. This is the only place **where** nobody can find us. 3. The museum **which** holds many secrets is heavily guarded. 4. He's the only person **who** knows the code. 5. She's the one **who/whom** we must protect. 6. There are many people **whose** lives are at risk. 7. **What** they want is redemption. **B: non-defining:** 1., 3.; **defining:** 2., 4., 5., 6.; **free:** 7; **C:** 4., 5.; **D:** 2., 5.

10. 2. Wearing, 3. to change, 4. to bring, 5. to do, 6. using, 7. to win, 8 throwing

11. 2. what he had done in training this week. 3. ...if/whether he would be playing the 4-4-2 system. 4 ...if/whether her was going to play the big man up front. 5. ...if/whether the players had celebrated after last week's performance.

12. 2. ...they had practised defending because they didn't want to concede any goals. 3. ...he was thinking about trying a new system. 4. ...the striker might play tomorrow, but he would decide later. 5. ...the players hadn't celebrated last week - they could celebrate when they win the league.

Kapitel 16

1. 2. The joke wasn't funny, so he wasn't laughing. 3. They don't exercise because it doesn't make a difference. 4. I haven't seen the film, which didn't get good reviews. 5. He didn't clean the bathroom because she hadn't reminded him. 6. You mustn't/needn't/don't have to believe everything you read! 7. I can't do it and I sure as hell won't do it!

2. 1. rarely, 2. hardly (ever), 3. never

3. 2. I never miss any fashion sales. 3. I rarely go out. 4. I hardly (ever) stay in. 5. I never meet new people. 6. I rarely miss the chance to meet new people.

4. 1. no, 2. nobody, 3. nothing, 4. no, 5. nowhere, 6. never

5. 2. I didn't know anybody in my town. 3. I wasn't doing anything all day. 4. There weren't any opportunities. 5. My friends weren't going anywhere with their lives. 6. I hadn't ever been abroad before.

Kapitel 17

1. 2. three hundred and fourteen, 3. one hundred and twenty-one, 4. two thousand and seventeen, 5. twelve thousand four hundred and eighty-three, 6. four hundred and seventy-three thousand eight hundred and seventy- one, 7. one million

2. 2. a few beers, 3. a dozen eggs, 4. thirty or so pancakes, 5. about 250 millilitres, 6. she's in her seventies

3. 1. 1st, 2. 3rd, 3. 5th, 4. 8th, 5. 17th, 6. 22nd, 7. 412th,

4. 2. 14th February, 3. 17th March, 4. 23rd April, 5. 2nd September, 6. 31st October, 7. 25th December

5. 2. fifty-nine BC, 3. ninety-nine AD, 4. eleven thirty-eight / eleven hundred and thirty-eight, 5. seventeen oh three / seventeen hundred and three, 6. nineteen sixty-six, 7. nineteen eighty-six, 8. twenty fifteen / two thousand and fifteen

6. 1. 0.02, 2. 5.96, 3. £13.23, 4. 19.047, 5. £444.55, 6. 13012.78

7. 1. Half, 2. quarters, 3. third, 4. sixth, 5. eighth, 6. fourteenth

8. 2. $\frac{3}{4}$, 3. $\frac{1}{3}$, 4. $\frac{1}{6}$, 5. $\frac{1}{8}$, 6. $\frac{1}{14}$

9. 2. C / triple, 3. A (three times), 4. E (twenty-eight times), 5. F (once), 6. D (quadrupled)

10. 2. Quarter to five. 3. Twenty-five past three. 4. Five to two. 5. Five past seven. 6. Nineteen past twelve.

11. 2. 04:45, 3. 03:25, 4. 13:55, 5. 19:05, 6. 12:19

12. 2. many, 3. not many, 4. few, 5. lots of/a lot of, 6. much, 7. a little, 8. not much, 9. little

13. 1. many, lots of, 2. much, little, 3. many, lot, 4. much, much

Bildnachweise

S. 3 weiße Tür: DiMmEr / Fotolia; **S. 4** Himmel mit Wolke: peshkova / Fotolia; **S. 5** : PONS GmbH /; **S. 6** Mind the Gap: sepiacheating / Fotolia; **S. 6** Neonschild: Karin Hildebrand Lau / shutterstock; **S. 6** Hund sitzt: Ron Chapple Studios / thinkstock; **S. 6** Hund springt: Global P / thinkstock; **S. 6** Junger Mann zeigt: LoloStock / Fotolia; **S. 6** Eisberg: niyazz / Fotolia; **S. 6** Buchstaben: bradcalkins / Fotolia; **S. 6** Bleilettern: hatmuth / Fotolia; **S. 6** Frau mit Nudelholz: Maxim Malevich / Fotolia; **S. 6** Satzlettern ‚Verb': B Calkins / shutterstock; **S. 6** Hände mit Fotos: Gabriele Rohde / Fotolia; **S. 7** Wahrsagerin: CREATISTA / thinkstock; **S. 7** Mann sitzt auf Boden: Edler von Rabenstein / Fotolia; **S. 7** Frau vor Telefon: El Gaucho / Fotolia; **S. 7** Huhn: andrewburgess / Fotolia; **S. 7** Schreibmaschine: Ivelin Radkov / shutterstock; **S. 7** Backstein und Kelle: filmfoto / thinkstock; **S. 7** Ablehnung: imageegami / Fotolia; **S. 7** Waage: Thomas / Fotolia; **S. 8, 9** Mind the Gap: sepiacheating / Fotolia; **S. 10** Junge: Subbotina Anna / shutterstock; **S. 10** Klavier: Christopher Hall / shutterstock; **S. 10** Gitarre: Nomad_Soul / shutterstock; **S. 10** Mond: beeboys / shutterstock; **S. 10** UBahn: Hemera Technologies / thinkstock; **S. 11** London Eye: Borut Trdina / istockphoto; **S. 11** Hund mit Hut: Best dog photo / shutterstock; **S. 11** Café: jakkapan / shutterstock; **S. 11** Spielfeld: Micha? Giedroj? / thinkstock; **S. 11** Öffnungszeiten: Chanyapatch Wongwiwat / shutterstock; **S. 12** Eselsohr: alfernec / shutterstock; **S. 12** Schauspieler: Igor Bulgarin / shutterstock; **S. 12** Hund: damedeeso / thinkstock; **S. 12** Fahrrad: 4Max / shutterstock; **S. 12** Stift: Alix Kreil / shutterstock; **S. 12** Adler: KarSol / shutterstock; **S. 12** Schirm: Christian Mueller / shutterstock; **S. 12** Lehrerin: El Nariz / shutterstock; **S. 13** Kochlöffel : amphaiwan / shutterstock; **S. 13** Kalender: toeytoey / shutterstock; **S. 13** Notfallwagen: Jaromir Chalabala / shutterstock; **S. 13** Katze: Alena Ozerova / shutterstock; **S. 13** Orange: Radu Bercan / shutterstock; **S. 13** Auto: lazyllama / shutterstock; **S. 13** Helikopter: razihusin / shutterstock; **S. 13** Ei: moodboard / thinkstock; **S. 14, 15** Buchstaben: bradcalkins / Fotolia; **S. 16** Frau Spanienflagge: franckreporter / istockphoto; **S. 16** Thanksgiving Schild: jenifoto / istockphoto; **S. 16** Freitag Kalender: YinYang / istockphoto; **S. 16** Karte Italien: omersukrugoksu / istockphoto; **S. 16** Madame Tussauds: okfoto / istockphoto; **S. 16** Bild Juni : Sportactive / istockphoto; **S. 17** Arzt: AlexRaths / istockphoto; **S. 17** Turnerin: KoKimk / istockphoto; **S. 17** Ehepaar: Oktay Ortakcioglu / istockphoto; **S. 17** Doktorhut: vkyryl / istockphoto; **S. 18** Fuchs: Edward Hasting-Evans / shutterstock; **S. 18** Füchse: artepicturas / Fotolia; **S. 18** Sandwiches: Moving Moment / shutterstock; **S. 18** Sandwich: Artenatura Images / shutterstock; **S. 18** Junge mit Drachen: ESB Professional / shutterstock; **S. 18** Wölfe: rogertrentham / thinkstock; **S. 18** Wolf: Nagel Photography / shutterstock; **S. 18** Erdbeeren: Olga Danylenko / shutterstock; **S. 18** Erdbeere: Aireo / shutterstock; **S. 18** Glas: Billion Photos / shutterstock; **S. 18** Gläser: Darkkong / shutterstock; **S. 18** Junge spielt mit Ball: x4wiz / shutterstock; **S. 19** tablet PC: Scanrail1 / shutterstock; **S. 19** Zucker: Sea Wave / shutterstock; **S. 19** Geld: Vladyslav Starozhylov / shutterstock; **S. 19** Tisch: MomentousPhotoVideo / thinkstock; **S. 19** Apfelsaft: Markus Mainka / shutterstock; **S. 19** Brot: mama_mia / shutterstock; **S. 19** Stift: Billion Photos / shutterstock; **S. 19** Zeitschriften: Bohbeh / shutterstock; **S. 19** Reis: perfectlab / shutterstock; **S. 19** Coffee: Dima Sobko / shutterstock; **S. 19** Zeitungen: aureliefrance / shutterstock; **S. 19** Pferd: Peera_stockfoto / shutterstock; **S. 20** Hose: eranicle / shutterstock; **S. 20** Brille: CASTALDOstudio.com / shutterstock; **S. 20** Schere: optimarc / shutterstock; **S. 20** Jeans: skynetphoto / shutterstock; **S. 20** Treppen: Photographee.eu / shutterstock; **S. 20** Kleidung: Kurmyshov / shutterstock; **S. 21** Pilotin: William Perugini / shutterstock; **S. 21** Arbeitsplatz: SFIO CRACHO / shutterstock; **S. 21** Auto: Dima Sidelnikov / shutterstock; **S. 21** junger Mann: Monkey Business Images / shutterstock; **S. 21** Fotograf: Godlikeart / shutterstock; **S. 21** Krankenschwester: Cherries / shutterstock; **S. 21** Schultafel: Cherries / shutterstock; **S. 22** Auto: Adkasai / shutterstock; **S. 22** Frau: Lopolo / shutterstock; **S. 22** Motorrad: Andrey Armyagov / shutterstock; **S. 22** Tom: mimagephotography / shutterstock; **S. 22** Charles: Alexander Kirch / shutterstock; **S. 22** Kinder: Pressmaster / shutterstock;

S. 22 Geburtstagskuchen: Jaktana phongphuek / shutterstock; **S. 22** Spielzeug: charles taylor / shutterstock; **S. 22** Katze: Chaikom / shutterstock; **S. 22** zwei Mädchen: Eugenio Marongiu / shutterstock; **S. 22** Eltern: michaeljung / thinkstock; **S. 22** zwei Smartphones: Kaspars Grinvalds / shutterstock; **S. 22** Ballon: monbibi / shutterstock; **S. 23** Ballon: monbibi / shutterstock; **S. 24, 25** Junger Mann zeigt: LoloStock / Fotolia; **S. 26** Mann, auf den gezeigt wird: Djomas / shutterstock; **S. 26** Mann zeigt von sich weg: Joana Lopes / shutterstock; **S. 27** Kamera: ronstik / shutterstock; **S. 27** Mann mit gebrochenem Bein: BlueSkyImage / shutterstock; **S. 27** Frau am Computer: Rawpixel.com / shutterstock; **S. 27** Mann und Frau trainieren: Halfpoint / shutterstock; **S. 27** Mann in kleinem Auto: Ollyy / shutterstock; **S. 27** Geschenke: Photographee.eu / shutterstock; **S. 27** kaputtes Smartphone: Take Photo / shutterstock; **S. 27** Leute schauen auf Smartphone: GaudiLab / shutterstock; **S. 28** Frau fotografiert: Daxiao Productions / shutterstock; **S. 29** Katze auf Sofa: liveostockimages / shutterstock; **S. 29** Freunde: Syda Productions / shutterstock; **S. 29** Gemüse: Yulia Grigoryeva / shutterstock; **S. 29** Finger mit Gesichtern: Victoria 1 / shutterstock; **S. 29** Hund : Polarpx / shutterstock; **S. 30** Children on football pitch: matimix / shutterstock; **S. 30** Salz und Pfeffer: George W. Bailey / shutterstock; **S. 30** junge Leute auf Stühlen: VGstockstudio / shutterstock; **S. 30** Frau schaut in Schaufenster: oneinchpunch / shutterstock; **S. 31** Frau probiert Sonnebrille an: guruXOX / shutterstock; **S. 31** Bücher: Yulia Grigoryeva / shutterstock; **S. 31** Junge mit leerer Schüssel: Prostock-studio / shutterstock; **S. 31** leere Geldbörse: B-D-S / shutterstock; **S. 32, 33** Eisberg: niyazz / Fotolia; **S. 34** Kalender: Brian A Jackson / shutterstock; **S. 34** Flughafen: Dabarti CGI / shutterstock; **S. 34** Aussicht aus Zugfenster: Eugenio Marongiu / shutterstock; **S. 34** Füße hoch: maxpetrov / shutterstock; **S. 35** Buch auf Tisch: Alix Kreil / shutterstock; **S. 35** Lavendelfeld: ronnybas / shutterstock; **S. 35** Café: Jacques PALUT / shutterstock; **S. 35** Wochenplaner: Rawpixel.com / shutterstock; **S. 35** Strand: Kent Weakley / shutterstock; **S. 36** Katze hinter Tür: Noskov Vladimir / shutterstock; **S. 36** Katze in Box: Africa Studio / shutterstock; **S. 36** Katze und Kind: AlikeYou / shutterstock; **S. 36** Katze in Liegestuhl: kuban_girl / shutterstock; **S. 36** Katze unter Liegestuhl: Papik / shutterstock; **S. 36** fliegender Fisch: stockphoto-graf / shutterstock; **S. 36** Katze schaut in Glas: Madhourse / shutterstock; **S. 36** Katze und Hund: VP Photo Studio / shutterstock; **S. 36** Katze wäscht sich: PAKULA PIOTR / shutterstock; **S. 37** Kinderzimmer: Photographee.eu / shutterstock; **S. 38** Bus auf Brücke: vitpho / istockphoto; **S. 38** Bus hält an: Maciej Bledowski / istockphoto; **S. 38** Kinder Busfenster: kali9 / istockphoto; **S. 38** purple girl bus: Kali Nine LLC / istockphoto; **S. 38** kids outside school: Yarinca / istockphoto; **S. 38** bus tunnel: PinkBadger / istockphoto; **S. 39** Schulbus: Stuart Monk / shutterstock; **S. 40** Hund springt: Ron Chapple Studios / thinkstock; **S. 41** Hund sitzt: Global P / thinkstock; **S. 42** happy face: Legend_art / shutterstock; **S. 42** active equipment: Stock-Asso / shutterstock; **S. 42** delicious: Ihor Voloshyn / shutterstock; **S. 42** difficult maths: Anthony Bolan / shutterstock; **S. 42** hungry: b7 / shutterstock; **S. 42** long: duchy / shutterstock; **S. 42** Baum: NE / shutterstock; **S. 42** Hände: Africa Studio / shutterstock; **S. 42** old car: mashurov / shutterstock; **S. 44** japanese flag: Fotogroove / shutterstock; **S. 44** thai flag: Globe Turner / shutterstock; **S. 44** french flag: Claudio Divizia / shutterstock; **S. 44** swiss flag: getfree / shutterstock; **S. 44** crying baby: Irina Rogova / shutterstock; **S. 44** rain window: Evgeny Atamanenko / shutterstock; **S. 44** dog snow: Ipedan / shutterstock; **S. 44** winning team: Ollyy / shutterstock; **S. 44** english flag: petch one / shutterstock; **S. 44** american flag: charnsitr / shutterstock; **S. 45** blackboard: Maridav / shutterstock; **S. 46** short road: Dmitry Guzhanin / shutterstock; **S. 46** goliath: Ron and Joe / shutterstock; **S. 46** tall building: Shahid Khan / shutterstock; **S. 46** scorpion: Protasov AN / shutterstock; **S. 46** pretty flowers: AppleZoomZoom / shutterstock; **S. 46** lazy dog: Annette Shaff / shutterstock; **S. 46** beach legs: ERainbow / shutterstock; **S. 46** funny: Sergey Furtaev / shutterstock; **S. 46** thinner: maradon 333 / shutterstock; **S. 47** Oktopus: Yellow Cat / shutterstock; **S. 47** Kobra: GraphicsRF / shutterstock; **S. 47** Auto: Tatiana Popova / shutterstock; **S. 47** Elefantenrüssel: Vaclav Volrab / shutterstock; **S. 47** Wal: Nature Art / shutterstock; **S. 47** Qualle: Prasanna Swaminathan / shutterstock; **S. 47** Bär: Daria Rybakova / shutterstock; **S. 48** burger: stockcreations / shutterstock; **S. 48** statue: jo Crebbin / shutterstock; **S. 48** woolly jumper: margostock / shutterstock; **S. 48** active girl: Halfpoint / shutterstock; **S. 48** windy dog: S Curtis / shutterstock; **S. 48** watch: NaiLAB / shutterstock; **S. 49** Paar auf Sofa: Patryk Kosmider / shutterstock; **S. 50, 51** Frau mit Nudelholz: Maxim Malevich / Fotolia; **S. 52** sloth: Janossy Gergely / shutterstock; **S. 53** smell man: Feel Photo Art / shutterstock; **S. 53** Zettel mit ‚L': Africa Studio / shutterstock; **S. 53** test: Joanna Dorota / shutterstock; **S. 53** clock: Andrey Savin / shutterstock; **S. 53** fence: Samuel Hakkinen / shutterstock; **S. 53** door: Artazum / shutterstock; **S. 54** singendes Mädchen: file404 / shutterstock; **S. 54** Uhr 09:10: Miyuki Satake / shutterstock; **S. 54** Opernsängerin: Kamil Macniak / shutterstock; **S. 54** Bierglas: Nikola Knezevic / shutterstock; **S. 54** Bierglas: Nikola Knezevic / shutterstock; **S. 54** Bierglas: Nikola Knezevic / shutterstock; **S. 54** singende Frau: liza54500 / shutterstock; **S. 54** Bild 4:0: Roma Koshel / shutterstock; **S. 54** Bild 3:0: Roma Koshel / shutterstock; **S. 54** Bild 1:0: Roma Koshel / shutterstock; **S. 54** Mann auf Berg: Sergey Nivens / shutterstock; **S. 54** Uhr 9:45: Miyuki Satake / shutterstock; **S. 54** kletterndes Kind: altanaka / shutterstock; **S. 54** Uhr 9:30: Miyuki Satake / shutterstock; **S. 54** Brief rechts: silm / shutterstock; **S. 54** Brief Mitte: Dmitry Karlov / shutterstock; **S. 54** Brief links: MagicDogWorkshop / shutterstock; **S. 54** Mann an Fassade: Evgeniy Zhukov / shutterstock; **S. 55** map uk: montree meejaroen / shutterstock; **S. 56** tea: sniegirova mariia / shutterstock; **S. 56** bake fail: Artur_eM / shutterstock; **S. 56** perfect cake: Lesya Dolyuk / shutterstock; **S. 57** proud woman: Borysevych.com / shutterstock; **S. 57** cakes in shop: wideonet / shutterstock; **S. 57** grandma rolling pin: Michael C. Gray / shutterstock; **S. 57** party: Olga Visavi / shutterstock; **S. 58, 59** Bleilettern: hatmuth / Fotolia; **S. 60** electric car: andrea lehmkuhl / shutterstock; **S. 60** thumbs up: Aha-Soft / shutterstock; **S. 60** thumbs up: Aha-Soft / shutterstock; **S. 60** thumbs up: Aha-Soft / shutterstock; **S. 60** thumbs down: Blur4265 / shutterstock; **S. 60** thumbs down: Blur4265 / shutterstock; **S. 61** off road car: Nneirda / shutterstock; **S. 61** thumbs up: Aha-Soft / shutterstock; **S. 61** thumbs up: Aha-Soft / shutterstock; **S. 61** thumbs up: Aha-Soft / shutterstock; **S. 61** thumbs down: Blur4265 / shutterstock; **S. 61** thumbs down: Blur4265 / shutterstock; **S. 62, 63** Satzlettern ‚Verb': B Calkins / shutterstock; **S. 64** Spiegelei: Magone / thinkstock; **S. 65** Cocktails: EugeneEL / thinkstock; **S. 65** Eiswürfel : Givaga / thinkstock; **S. 66** Herzen Leti i: stasknop / Fotolia; **S. 67** couple kiss: Karuka / shutterstock; **S. 67** speed dating: Sam72 / shutterstock; **S. 67** breakfast: vm2002 / shutterstock; **S. 67** chalk stickmen: Fiesfive / shutterstock; **S. 68** cow: Dudarev Mikhail / shutterstock; **S. 69** broken egg: mokokomo / shutterstock; **S. 70** Post-It bunt: Lucky_Guy / thinkstock; **S. 70** Post-It bunt: Lucky_Guy / thinkstock; **S. 70** Uhr: Wasant / shutterstock; **S. 70** toilet: Yuksal Sarıkhanli / shutterstock; **S. 70** partners: Ms VectorPlus / shutterstock; **S. 70** no phones: Alexey Pushkin / shutterstock; **S. 70** board: Kitch Bain / shutterstock; **S. 70** study: Denis Maliugin / shutterstock; **S. 70** fast food: nikolae / shutterstock; **S. 71** blackboard: Vinne / shutterstock; **S. 71** teaching class: solgas / shutterstock; **S. 73** clock head: PhotoMediaGroup / shutterstock; **S. 73** bar drinks: thanosquest / shutterstock; **S. 73** messy baby: Val Shevchenko / shutterstock; **S. 73** sock drawer: Ken Tannenbaum / shutterstock; **S. 73** empty pocket: ThefotosoloNo1 / shutterstock; **S. 73** map phone: Alexey Boldin / shutterstock; **S. 74** man sleeping bag: Galyna Andrushko / shutterstock; **S. 74** Zielscheibe: brandstock / shutterstock; **S. 74** fire: pockygallery / shutterstock; **S. 74** penknife: JR T / shutterstock; **S. 74** ropes: Anna.zabella / shutterstock; **S. 74** home sweet: Kunst Bilder / shutterstock; **S. 74** kid plane: Sunny studio / shutterstock; **S. 74** bow arrow: quka / shutterstock; **S. 75** Cupcakes: RuthBlack / thinkstock; **S. 76** ski jump: Igor Chus / shutterstock; **S. 76** roof rack ski: Cory Woodruff / shutterstock; **S. 76** slalom: Ruslan Kudrin / shutterstock; **S. 76** thermometer cold: Gary Whitton / shutterstock; **S. 76** trees danger: gdefilip / shutterstock; **S. 77** apres ski: Dinga / shutterstock; **S. 77** old skool skier: Everett Collection / shutterstock; **S. 77** snowboard equipment: Dmytro Vietrov / shutterstock; **S. 77** spa: PhotoMediaGroup / shutterstock **S. 78** rose: Vagastar / shutterstock; **S. 78** date night: chrisdorney / shutterstock; **S. 78** dinner oysters: Rawpixel.com / shutterstock; **S. 78** texting: GaudiLab / shutterstock; **S. 78** glass slipper: sha aku / shutterstock; **S. 78** Geldautomat loftyty e / shutterstock; **S. 80, 81** Neonschild: Karin Hildebrand Lau / shutterstock; **S. 82, 83** alte laufschuhe: langvzsolt / thinkstock; **S. 84, 85** Hände mit Fotos: Gabriele Rohde / fotolia; **S. 86** walk: Binkski / shutterstock; **S. 86** destroy: Kunst Bilder / shutterstock; **S. 86** hate: totallypic / shutterstock; **S. 86** kiss: puthithons / shutterstock; **S. 86** copy: Carlos Rojas V / shutterstock; **S. 86** need: TungCheung / shutterstock; **S. 86** try: Ionut Catalin Parvu / shutterstock; **S. 86** stop: Archiwiz / shutterstock; **S. 86** start: Delpixel / shutterstock; **S. 87** Kinder backen: gysc4ka / thinkstock; **S. 87** Frau hält Kopf: Ollyy / shutterstock; **S. 87** EC-Gerät: alice-photo / shutterstock; **S. 87** Fahrradfahren: Daxiao Productions / shutterstock; **S. 87** zeigen: Yuganov Konstantin / shutterstock; **S. 87** Bücher: Thomas Bethge / shutterstock; **S. 87** Ohr: Arthimedes / shutterstock; **S. 87** trinken: MsMaria / shutterstock; **S. 87** Go!: Artulina / shutterstock; **S. 87** fangen: SumanBhaumik / shutterstock; **S. 88** beach: Sunny studio / shutterstock; **S. 88** cupcake: SnerSo / shutterstock; **S. 88** donkey: Authentic travel / shutterstock; **S. 88** beers: Africa Studio / shutterstock; **S. 88** old book: spaxiax / shutterstock; **S. 88** fairytale: KristinaSh / shutterstock; **S. 88** fruit: Netfalls Remy Musser / shutterstock; **S. 89** sofa girl: runzelkorn / shutterstock; **S. 89** english breakfast: Monkey Business Images / shutterstock; **S. 89** microwave: Monkey Business Images / shutterstock; **S. 89** feet up: bikeriderlondon / shutterstock; **S. 89** walk dog: Andrea Obzerova / shutterstock; **S. 89** meditate: Kite_rin / shutterstock; **S. 89** travel tube: Halfpoint / shutterstock; **S. 89** bed feet: Olga Danylenko / shutterstock; **S. 90, 91** Schulbus Schnee: onepony / fotolia; **S. 92, 93** Musiknoten: tassel78 / shutterstock; **S. 94** Fahrradweg: Ingram Publishing / thinkstock; **S. 96** Mann und Frau streiten: VGstockstudio / shutterstock; **S. 96** delays: Mr Doomits / shutterstock; **S. 96** bubble gum: Shvaygert Ekaterina / shutterstock; **S. 96** knitting: Joanna B / shutterstock; **S. 96** bus stop sign: Aran Kaewkhammul / shutterstock; **S. 96** cigar: BlueOrange Studio / shutterstock; **S. 97** waiting: Andrew Babble / shutterstock; **S. 97** bell: picton / shutterstock; **S. 97** lawn mower: Marcin Pawinski / shutterstock; **S. 97** clean plates: Carlos andre Santos / shutterstock; **S. 98** save the date: Ekaphon maneechot / shutterstock; **S. 98** found money: JaysonPhotography / shutterstock; **S. 98** london: SEREE YINDEE / shutterstock; **S. 98** find keys: cunaplus / shutterstock; **S. 101** ET: 360b / shutterstock; **S. 101** messy bed: Margie Hurwich / shutterstock; **S. 101** old couple: Laszlo66 / shutterstock; **S. 101** coffee hands: Africa Studio / shutterstock; **S. 101** crying child: Kamelia Ilieva / shutterstock; **S. 101** fish: Nataliia Zhekova / shutterstock; **S. 101** map couple car: wavebreakmedia / shutterstock; **S. 101** bench friends: Forster Forest / shutterstock; **S. 104** Freunde: View Apart / shutterstock; **S. 104** fat guy: Creativa Images / shutterstock; **S. 104** crying woman: JPagetRFPhotos / shutterstock; **S. 104** not listening: ESB Professional / shutterstock; **S. 104** Mann mit Handtuch: Jinga / shutterstock; **S. 104** drinking: Milan Ilic Photographer / shutterstock; **S. 104** paint: Coffeemill / shutterstock; **S. 104** mountain climbers: Jakraphong Photography / shutterstock; **S. 106** shake hands: thodonal88 / shutterstock; **S. 106** bed lie: VITA PIX / shutterstock; **S. 106** wife phone: Di Studio / shutterstock; **S. 106** stressed: Freedom My wing / shutterstock; **S. 107** Chapter 4: MyImages – Micha / shutterstock; **S. 107** PC: Rawpixel.com / shutterstock; **S. 107** best seller: ESB Basic / shutterstock; **S. 107** sleep typewriter: zoff / shutterstock; **S. 108, 109** Schreibmaschine: Ivelin Radkov / shutterstock; **S. 110** bat hang: Filip Serban / shutterstock; **S. 110** pow: NoraVector / shutterstock; **S. 110** spider logo: dean bertoncelj / shutterstock; **S. 110** cinema couple: Syda

Productions / shutterstock; **S. 110** super girl: llaszlo / shutterstock; **S. 110** bat car: 1000 words / shutterstock; **S. 110** strong woman: Nomad_Soul / shutterstock; **S. 110** fire chest: Sergey Nivens / shutterstock; **S. 110** spiderman climbing: enchanted_fairy / shutterstock; **S. 111** lego batman: Bubbers BB / shutterstock; **S. 111** lego superman: Bubbers BB / shutterstock; **S. 112** ballet shoes: Roman Prishenko / shutterstock; **S. 112** calendar: Fabrizio Misson / shutterstock; **S. 112** warm up ballet: Alexander Y / shutterstock; **S. 112** slice of pie: ilolab / shutterstock; **S. 112** night party: vchal / shutterstock; **S. 112** burger milkshake: Global2016 / shutterstock; **S. 113** flying: Ljupco Smokovski / shutterstock; **S. 113** balancing: Sergey Nivens / shutterstock; **S. 113** getting angry: pattang / shutterstock; **S. 113** hanging: FUN FUN PHOTO / shutterstock; **S. 113** fighting: Danomyte / shutterstock; **S. 116, 117** Wahrsagerin: CREATISTA / thinkstock; **S. 118** Agenda : Maxx Satori / shutterstock; **S. 120** warm man: domin_domin / istockphoto; **S. 120** sunburn: JohnnyGreig / istockphoto; **S. 120** wellies: cjp / istockphoto; **S. 120** umbrella: fstop123 / istockphoto; **S. 120** sunglasses: Alija / istockphoto; **S. 120** scarf and gloves: serazetdinov / istockphoto; **S. 121** rain: JuSun / istockphoto; **S. 121** snow: JuSun / istockphoto; **S. 121** sun: Robin_Hoood / istockphoto; **S. 122** dance?: Mlenny / istockphoto; **S. 122** dinner: kieferpix / istockphoto; **S. 122** proposing: Ridofranz / istockphoto; **S. 123** bored girl: BraunS / istockphoto; **S. 123** airport man: anyaberkut / istockphoto; **S. 123** dog sofa: NWphotoguy / istockphoto; **S. 123** 3 kids: Image Source / istockphoto; **S. 124, 125** Hintergrund Papier: ESB Professional / shutterstock; **S. 126** Giraffe: Alex Hubenov / shutterstock; **S. 126** Hintergrund Papier: ESB Professional / shutterstock; **S. 127** cow milk: Boogich / istockphoto; **S. 127** empty bowl: steve-goacher / istockphoto; **S. 127** party room: StudioThreeDots / istockphoto; **S. 127** tv socks: AlessandroZocc / istockphoto; **S. 128** lawnmower close up: the_guitar_mann / istockphoto; **S. 128** bored at work: grinvalds / istockphoto; **S. 128** sleeping after party: Yuri_Arcurs / istockphoto; **S. 128** fat runner: Nastco / istockphoto; **S. 129** arrivals: alice-photo / istockphoto; **S. 129** watching game: andresr / istockphoto; **S. 129** dirty boots: klikk / istockphoto; **S. 129** sleep plane: kasto80 / istockphoto; **S. 130** Abendessen mit Wein: Thomas Jackson / GettyImages; **S. 131** Filmklappe: Alex Staroseltsev / shutterstock; **S. 132** kicking seat: craftvision / istockphoto; **S. 132** burnt chicken: Oktay Ortakcioglu / istockphoto; **S. 132** dirty dog: adogslifephoto / istockphoto; **S. 132** strict teacher: Andreyuu / istockphoto; **S. 132** bored couple: lisegagne / istockphoto; **S. 133** Holzbesteck: Sasajo / Fotolia; **S. 133** Holzbesteck: Sasajo / Fotolia; **S. 134** vegas lights: LPETTET / istockphoto; **S. 134** cheers: Instants / istockphoto; **S. 134** aces: DeReGe / istockphoto; **S. 134** hands: TuelekZa / istockphoto; **S. 135** vegas sign: marco2polo / istockphoto; **S. 135** bored gamblers: RoBeDeRo / istockphoto; **S. 135** bad cards: KLH49 / istockphoto; **S. 135** wedding vegas: littleny / istockphoto; **S. 137** Huhn: andrewburgess / Fotolia; **S. 138** indoor skier: Alija / istockphoto; **S. 138** beach chair: maxsaf / istockphoto; **S. 138** soup: Panaroid / istockphoto; **S. 138** snow cars: MarianVejcik / istockphoto; **S. 138** igloo man: Nataliia_Makarova / istockphoto; **S. 138** snow bus: aetb / istockphoto; **S. 138** sledges: lorenzo104 / istockphoto; **S. 138** snowman: Mari / istockphoto; **S. 139** girl: Slphotography / istockphoto; **S. 140** toothache: Anetlanda / istockphoto; **S. 140** kids black and white: zizulhalmi / istockphoto; **S. 140** snails: LauriPatterson / istockphoto; **S. 140** open window: sUs_angel / istockphoto; **S. 141** volcano town: loca4motion / istockphoto; **S. 141** snow climb: thinair28 / istockphoto; **S. 141** volcano tour: Natalia Moroz / istockphoto; **S. 142** Händchenhalten: Pavinee Chareonpanich / shutterstock; **S. 143** man thinking: PIKSEL / istockphoto; **S. 143** money pounds: Andrew_Howe / istockphoto; **S. 143** red car: lisegagne / istockphoto; **S. 144** Betrunkener: Ljupco Smokovski / Fotolia; **S. 145** hungover man: kieferpix / istockphoto; **S. 146** book on beach: stock_colors / istockphoto; **S. 146** suncream sun: DmitrijsDmitrijevs / istockphoto; **S. 147** rain window: percds / istockphoto; **S. 147** cliff jump: EpicStockMedia / istockphoto; **S. 147** tango dance: JoseASReyes / istockphoto; **S. 147** cheap flights: glegorly / istockphoto; **S. 148, 149** Peru: aaabbbccc / shutterstock; **S. 150, 151** Backstein und Kelle: filmfoto / thinkstock; **S. 152, 153** Flammen: Potapov Alexander / shutterstock; **S. 154** barbeque: mphillips007 / istockphoto; **S. 155** sausage: Damocless / istockphoto; **S. 155** apron man: emyerson / istockphoto; **S. 155** cocktails: knape / istockphoto; **S. 157, 158** Satzzeichen: donatas1205 / shutterstock; **S. 159** bad parking: killerbayer / istockphoto; **S. 159** tired worker: lisegagne / istockphoto; **S. 159** roundabout: Miranda1066 / istockphoto; **S. 159** Dull sign: northlightimages / istockphoto; **S. 160** Frau vor Telefon: Edler von Rabenstein / Fotolia; **S. 161** Mann sitzt auf Boden: El Gaucho / Fotolia; **S. 162** dog carrot: damedeeso / istockphoto; **S. 162** dog bed: Chalabala / istockphoto; **S. 163** turtle flying: be_low / istockphoto; **S. 163** tank: mtreasure / istockphoto; **S. 163** turtle climbing: denisgo / istockphoto; **S. 164** dog stick: damedeeso / istockphoto; **S. 165** Lost dog: Vector Pixel Star / shutterstock; **S. 166** stop: ollo / istockphoto; **S. 166** drive carefully: davincidig / istockphoto; **S. 166** safety: Lurin / istockphoto; **S. 166** no left: bigdoug2005 / istockphoto; **S. 166** drive safely: liorpt / istockphoto; **S. 166** changes: scibak / istockphoto; **S. 166** thank you: jcarillet / istockphoto; **S. 166** don't walk: absolut_100 / istockphoto; **S. 167** Auto innen: atibody photo / shutterstock; **S. 168** Herz 3: alisafarov / shutterstock; **S. 168** Herz 2: Sanphoto69 / shutterstock; **S. 168** Herz 1: Jiri Hera / shutterstock; **S. 168** Herz 6 : Studio_G / shutterstock; **S. 168** Herz 4: YolLusZam1802 / shutterstock; **S. 168** Herz 5: Dinga / shutterstock; **S. 169** writing book: peshkov / istockphoto; **S. 169** bra: alekleks / istockphoto; **S. 169** broken heart: grafvision / istockphoto; **S. 169** heart book: aluxum / istockphoto; **S. 169** legs: AntonioGuillem / istockphoto; **S. 170, 171** Thunfisch: holbox / shutterstock; **S. 172** security: iunderhill / istockphoto; **S. 172** light door: MATJAZ SLANIC / istockphoto; **S. 172** book key: deepblue4you / istockphoto; **S. 172** red eyes: Plus69 / istockphoto; **S. 173** Cowboys: CREATISTA / shutterstock; **S. 173** Männer reiten: typhoonski / istockphoto; **S. 173** Cowgirl : Maridav / shutterstock; **S. 174** griechische Maske: Repina Valeriya / shutterstock; **S. 174** Amphitheater: muratart / shutterstock; **S. 174, 175** griechisches Theater Vektor: Thumbelina / shutterstock; **S. 176** press conf. Man: razihusin / istockphoto; **S. 177** microphones: wellphoto / istockphoto; **S. 178, 179** Frauen: imageegami / Fotolia; **S. 180** runners: pixdeluxe / istockphoto; **S. 180** funny: Sergey Furtaev / shutterstock; **S. 180** hungrige Menschen: Syda Productions / shutterstock; **S. 181** clean toilet: djedzura / istockphoto; **S. 181** thumbs down: Phoenixns / istockphoto; **S. 181** can't do it: BrianAJackson / istockphoto; **S. 181** magazines: David_Ahn / istockphoto; **S. 184** vektor landschaft: Diane Labombarbe / istockphoto; **S. 185** lonely drinking: KatarzynaBialasiewicz / istockphoto; **S. 185** house of cards: LapwingMedia / istockphoto; **S. 185** crowd: Maxiphoto / istockphoto; **S. 185** bored on sofa: g-stockstudio / istockphoto; **S. 185** no jobs: Carolyn Franks / shutterstock; **S. 185** passport: gashgeron / istockphoto; **S. 186, 187** Waage: Thomas / Fotolia; **S. 188** 121: Oleg Kozlov / shutterstock; **S. 188** calculator: catenarymedia / istockphoto; **S. 188** 473871: Digiphoto / istockphoto; **S. 188** 314: burwellphotography / istockphoto; **S. 188** 2017: glebchik / istockphoto; **S. 188** 28: mbbirdy / istockphoto; **S. 188** million: aquarius83men / istockphoto; **S. 189** liquid: RapidEye / istockphoto; **S. 189** pancakes: ChristiTolbert / istockphoto; **S. 189** eggs: Avesun / shutterstock; **S. 189** beers: Erdosain / istockphoto; **S. 189** ältere Dame: gradyreese / istockphoto; **S. 189** ducks: Valengilda / istockphoto; **S. 190** Treppen: Nikada / istockphoto; **S. 191** pumpkin: ryasick / istockphoto; **S. 191** coconuts: joji / istockphoto; **S. 191** Hamlet skull: vasiliki / istockphoto; **S. 191** St. Patrick: terra24 / istockphoto; **S. 191** new years resolutions: catherine_jones / istockphoto; **S. 191** love fingers: Xesai / istockphoto; **S. 191** socks: Artfoliophoto / istockphoto; **S. 194** Melone 8 Teile : Adrian Costea / thinkstock; **S. 194** Pizza 6 Teile: Elenadesign / shutterstock; **S. 194** choc. Cake: elikatseva / istockphoto; **S. 194** donut: stacey_newman / istockphoto; **S. 194** lemon: anna1311 / istockphoto; **S. 194** apple timer: Devenorr / istockphoto; **S. 195** Inbox 12: tomeng / istockphoto; **S. 195** Inbox 4: subman / istockphoto; **S. 195** little heart: andrej_k / istockphoto; **S. 195** kid in front blackboard: BrianAJackson / istockphoto; **S. 195** sandwich: atiatiati / istockphoto; **S. 195** 8 ice cream: ALEAIMAGE / istockphoto; **S. 195** fingers: simplytheyu / istockphoto; **S. 196** 4:45: nemar74 / istockphoto; **S. 196** 2:30: thavornc / istockphoto; **S. 196** 12:19: typo-graphics / istockphoto; **S. 196** 1:55: gmutlu / istockphoto; **S. 196** 7:05: SrdjanPav / istockphoto; **S. 196** 3:25: Nikada / istockphoto; **S. 197** day/night: Mike Pellinni / shutterstock; **S. 198** Meer: abadonian / istockphoto; **S. 198** jellybeans: daniel_wiedemann / istockphoto; **S. 199** ham: GOSPHOTODESIGN / istockphoto; **S. 199** cheese: jjwithers / istockphoto; **S. 199** wine bottles: Africa Studio / shutterstock; **S. 199** grapes: jannoon028 / shutterstock; **S. 200, 201** Kinder: RichVintage / istockphoto